A Place for All

The publishing team included Steven C. McGlaun, development editor; Lorraine Kilmartin, reviewer; prepress and manufacturing coordinated by the production departments of Saint Mary's Press.

Printed in the United States of America

2305

ISBN 978-0-88489-972-3

Library of Congress Cataloging-in-Publication Data

Barone, John, 1961–
   A place for all : ministry for youth with special needs / John Barone.
   p. cm.
ISBN 978-0-88489-972-3 (pbk.)
   1. Children with mental disabilities—Education. 2. Christian education of children with mental disabilities. 3. Monarch School (Houston, Tex.) I. Title.
LC4601.B328 2008
268'.432087—dc22

2008003816

A Place for All

Ministry for Youth with Special Needs

John Barone, M.A.

The Monarch School

Houston, Texas

Saint Mary's Press®

Dedication

To Marty, mentor and friend, who sees the beautiful butterfly in all of us, even before it emerges, and gently coaxes us to take flight.

Author Acknowledgments

One person did not write this book. It is a rich and varied collection of the ideas, beliefs, and practices of many, both at The Monarch School and in Catholic education and youth ministry.

Thanks to all the Monarch faculty, parents, and students for their support and contributions to this work, especially to the leadership team of The Monarch School, as follows:

- Dr. Marty Webb, for outstanding leadership in her role as head of The Monarch School, guiding us all in our mission to provide an innovative, therapeutic education for children with neurological differences.
- Dr. Neal Sarahan, Monarch Challenger Program director, whose curiosity and love of learning permeate all the work we do, transforming the lives of the children we serve.
- Dr. Debrah Hall, Monarch Apprentice Program director, whose passion for helping children reach their full potential keeps us all focused on the most important priority: our students.

Much gratitude also to Eugene Webb, author, psychotherapist, and cofounder of The Monarch School, for his wise counsel, humorous support, and caring friendship. Unbelievable!

Special thanks to Laurie Delgatto for her important role in the development of this book. Thank you for your advocacy, guidance, and care.

Finally, a big thank you to my family: my wife, Susie; my parents, Alice and Richard; and all the members of the Barone clan for their encouragement and support.

Contents

About The Monarch School and the Author

The Monarch School, in Houston, Texas, is dedicated to providing an innovative, therapeutic education for children with neurological differences. The school is committed to serving the special education needs of children in the community by offering a unique, therapeutic learning environment where active minds are challenged, all are treated with respect and dignity, learning is a joy, and wisdom is the outcome.

The school's unique blend of psychology and education provides a highly individualized program to meet the emotional, social, and academic needs of each child. Monarch has outreach services for the larger community through its Learning Center and its Diagnostic Clinic. The Monarch School also has a Life Academy, teaching students about the business of life through entrepreneurship and student-based businesses.

John Barone received his bachelor of arts degree in religious education from the University of St. Thomas in Houston, and his master of arts degree in private school administration from the Institute for Catholic Educational Leadership at the University of San Francisco. John has extensive background in adolescent development, Catholic education and youth ministry, workshop facilitation, and teaching students with neurological differences. He serves as the director of The Monarch Learning Center, which is The Monarch School's response to the urgent call of parents, teachers, administrators, medical professionals, and mental health professionals hungry for the skills and knowledge to empower them to transform the lives of students with special needs.

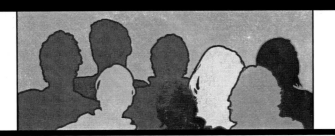

Foreword

In a recent family counseling session with the parents and twin sisters of Kurt, a fourteen-year-old boy, I asked who his favorite teacher was at school. He replied without hesitation, "Mr. Jennings, my math teacher."

"Because he really knows his math?" Kurt's dad asked provocatively.

"No," smiled Kurt, "because he knows me."

"Oh," offered his mom, "he knows you remember to do your homework."

"No," stated Kurt, "he remembers that I can't do math unless I repeat the numbers in my head."

That was a golden moment for everyone in the room, not just because Kurt's response was so revealing but also more because of his delightful paradigm shift: a sudden change in focus from what he does to who he is. It was a shift from how math is performed to an appreciation by his teacher of who Kurt is. That moment awakened Kurt's whole family to appreciate how important it is that he be "found out" by teachers dedicated not just to teaching but also to how students with special needs learn.

My grandma used to say we all live with two fears: the fear we will be found out, and the fear we won't. She meant we all live with the terror that our unique personalities, our atypical looks, our imperfect bodies, our origins, our quirky ways, and our interests, tastes, and learning styles will disqualify us from inclusion in and acceptance by the group. At the same time, we live with the hope that those same unique qualities will be discovered, honored, and welcomed into the group. We want to be like others in the group, and we want to be different from them—both as invitations to be part of the group.

How do we accomplish being the same and different, simultaneously, in a learning experience? Kurt tells us the secret:

> "I want to learn what everyone else here is learning, but I need to experience it my way, the way that makes sense to me, so I can make sense of it. And if our teacher can catch on to how each of us learns differently by creating experiences that invite our differences, then we can have a group experience that includes all of us."

I am in awe of this kid! Just as I am in awe of the staff of The Monarch School, who have provided in this book a bridge between Kurt's wish and the wish of religious educators who are challenged by challenged kids.

These educators have brought together four major themes crucial to working with young people in religious contexts, as follows:

- Education is not about reciting information and then testing for regurgitation skills.
- Teaching is about creating vivid, personal, and dramatic opportunities for all in the classroom—teachers included—to have personally unique responses relevant to their current lives.
- Learning is about doing, comparing, experiencing emotional drama, discusing, asking, wondering, and differing about life in the context of faith.
- Answers and outcomes are not nearly as important or riveting as the process of personal awakening to one's own relevance in the group and confirmation of oneself before God.

The experts at The Monarch School approach these issues with brilliance, humor, and candor, speaking as learners as much as they do as teachers. That is the genius of this book: the work of dealing with our challenged youth combines being a constant learner of "who" with the ever-changing crafting of "what."

Thank you, Kurt, for your incisive, adolescent wisdom: "Because you know me, I can learn it."

Respectfully,

Eugene Webb, LPC, psychotherapist, cofounder of The Monarch School
Houston, Texas
Fall 2007

1

Such Is the Reign

Great crowds had been following the Master, Jesus, for some time, and on one occasion, parents began to bring their children to him to be blessed. As the parents pressed around him, their eyes were filled with joy and hope, believing that the Master's touch could transform the lives of their children.

The Apostles, seeing the great crush of people surrounding Jesus, began to criticize the parents harshly, but Jesus stopped them:

"No! 'Suffer little children, and forbid them not, to come unto me' (Matthew 19:14; King James Version); don't stop them. Don't you know that the Reign of God belongs to such as these?"

And so the children gathered around him. He touched them, blessed them, and prayed over them. The parents were overjoyed, and the children beamed when he looked at them.

Except for Sarah. When it was her turn to see Jesus, Sarah didn't return his loving gaze. She kept looking at a shiny green stone in her hand, turning it over and over. "What do you have there, Sarah?" Jesus gently asked, as he reached out to touch the stone. "Don't!" She pulled her hand sharply away.

"Sarah," the Master said compassionately, "If you want me to bless you, you're going to have to look me in the eye, and put that stone down."

"No!" Sarah refused.

Jesus shook his head in disappointment and called for the parents. "I'm sorry, but I can't bless her if she won't even look at me. She's disobedient and refuses to follow my instructions. And she's obviously not gaining anything by being here with me. All she cares about is that green stone. Please take her home." The parents sighed and sadly made their way through the crowd with their little girl.

The next child, Joshua, smiled at Jesus, looked him right in the eye, and wrapped his arms around Jesus' neck. Jesus was pleased with this little boy and began to bless him. But while the Master was blessing him, Joshua began to make hooting noises. Jesus said, "Please stop that, Joshua; you're a little boy, not an owl!" All the other children began to laugh except Joshua, but at least he stopped hooting for a little while.

Then Joshua's head began to twitch. Then he hooted again. Jesus called for the parents. "I'm sorry, but Joshua's noises and twitches are disrupting the blessings. It's obvious that he can control it, because he stopped when I asked him to. But then a few minutes later he started hooting again. Joshua is making the other children uncomfortable with all these strange noises and twitches. I'm really sorry, but I don't think he can stay." Joshua and his family looked humiliated as they walked away.

Martha was next, but just as she was walking up, Benjamin was so excited to see Jesus that he pushed his way past her and knocked her down. Martha was so upset that she began to scream uncontrollably. She threw herself down on the ground, yelling, "It's not fair! I was next! It's not his turn! I hate that boy! Wahhhh!"

Jesus signaled to both sets of parents, who picked up their children and took them away, avoiding the accusing eyes of the other parents. Martha's screams could still be heard in the distance as Jesus smiled and welcomed the next appropriately behaving child.

Does this story ring true to you? Does this sound like the Jesus you know? When Jesus said, ". . . for it is to such as these that the kingdom of heaven belongs" (Matthew 19:14), do you suppose there was an unrecorded qualifier like the following: ". . . except those with attention differences, social development problems, self-regulation issues, physical and verbal tics, mood disorders, and any other neurological difference that would affect their functioning."

Probably not. Jesus clearly made every effort to reach out to those who were different, marginalized, or troubled. Jesus would not have turned these young people away. You may be familiar with the words from the King James Version of the Bible, "Suffer little children . . . to come unto me" (Matthew 19:14). Jesus used the word *suffer* in the sense of "to permit." He was asking the Apostles to give the children permission to approach him.

Then why do young people with special needs so frequently find it difficult to approach our religious education and youth ministry programs? Why do some of us find it difficult to welcome them? This book is about challenged youth, but it is also about challenged teachers and challenged parents.

Our Hearts Are in the Right Place, but Our Children Aren't

Some faith communities work hard at including all God's children. But sadly you often won't find young people with autism, Tourette's syndrome, or severe attention problems in religious education classrooms. If these young people are present, they are too often gathered in one special room where they may be supervised but may not be catechized.

It's not because faith communities don't want to include these young people. I trust that the spirit of our pastors, directors of religious education (DREs), youth ministry coordinators, and catechists is one of welcoming and inclusion. Then why isn't it happening? Following are some possible reasons:

"It's Too Hard"

I've done some hard work in my life. At my first job at a fast-food restaurant, I was lucky enough to be assigned the task of emptying and scrubbing the grease bins. I later worked in a non-air-conditioned sheet metal factory, where I fashioned and assembled ductwork. Then as an electrician's apprentice, I crawled through hot attics to install and repair wiring.

I'm no stranger to hard work, but I didn't really know what hard work was until I came to The Monarch School. It's been the hardest and the best job I've ever had. The Monarch School was founded in 1997 on a dream, with no money, no space, no classrooms, no faculty, and no students. The school was a response to a critical need in the community to provide an innovative, therapeutic education for children with neurological differences. The community responded with tremendous support!

In the first year, there were six teachers, one part-time psychologist, two consultants, and twenty-three students with various neurological disorders, such as autism, bipolar disorder, severe language learning disabilities, and Tourette's syndrome. But we knew even then that at Monarch, working with kids wasn't about labels. It was about knowing and working with each child as an individual, unique in the universe.

The neurological differences of our students have affected their learning, as well as their social and emotional development. It is common for them to come to us having been subjected to daily ridicule and rejection. Many are seriously at risk for school dropout, unemployment, and even suicide. For those who are autistic, research suggests they have little chance of falling in love, marrying, or having a family. Our desire is to help young people achieve goals that others thought they would never be able to achieve.

We are now in our eleventh year and are getting ready to move into our permanent home, a beautiful complex on 10 acres. We have established a unique therapeutic program that is a coordinated blend of educational and psychological services. We have outreach services to the greater Houston community through our Learning Center and our Diagnostic Clinic. We have a Life Academy, teaching students about the business of life through entrepreneurship and student-based businesses.

The Monarch program is not modeled on any other program. It is original, innovative, and constantly improving. Monarch exists today because we believe every child deserves to learn, be respected, and experience joy. Monarch will exist tomorrow for the same reasons. It will exist because we constantly strive to better meet the needs of the students who physically find their way to our school and emotionally find their way to our hearts.

I began my Monarch adventure in a self-contained classroom with six boys. Some had autism, some had Tourette's syndrome, and all had difficulty controlling their emotions and following directions. Meltdowns were a daily occurrence, with lots of crying and screaming. Sometimes the students would all melt at the same time. It was . . . challenging.

On his first day, a new student I will call Michael refused to come into the classroom. For several days he stood outside the room, ignoring my attempts to communicate with him. So I just spent quiet time near him, trying periodically to connect. Finally after several days, we had a breakthrough. When I asked him, "How are you today, Michael?" he finally spoke to me. He looked me right in the eye and said, "Why don't you just go to hell?"

I was delighted that he engaged me, and from that point on, things got better. We communicated. He joined us in the classroom and began the long, hard work of learning how to be a student in a classroom, how to connect with others socially, and how to regulate his emotions. From day one we chose not to focus on Michael's obscenities or other provocative behaviors, instead paying attention to times when he chose to engage us and coaching him as he slowly developed his relationship skills. In the same way, Jesus chose not to focus on the weaknesses of the people the community rejected but instead accepted them as they were and encouraged them to take ownership of their struggles.

I've kept up with Michael and have been delighted to see him continue to grow in the expert care of my colleagues. Awhile ago I saw him at a Monarch dance. Throughout our work together, Michael had never been comfortable with physical affection. But when I saw him at this dance, I thought I'd take a chance. I told him it was great to see him, and I asked him for permission to give him a hug. He looked up at me cautiously, thought about it for a moment, and then said, "Yeah, I guess that would be all right." I couldn't have been prouder.

The concern about the difficulty of working with young people with special needs is valid. Sometimes it's hard. But when we step out of our comfort zones and connect with young people in a spirit of love, miracles can happen.

"I'm Not Trained for This"

Each summer I direct the DeBusk Enrichment Center for Academically Talented Scholars (DECATS), a three-week enrichment program for gifted kids. The mission of the program is to influence the leaders of tomorrow to develop a commitment to use their gifts to serve others in a spirit of humility. Our motto is "'Better at' does not mean 'better than.'"

In DECATS we deliberately seek out "twice exceptional" young people: kids who are very bright and who also have special challenges. One such scholar, a fourth grader I will call Carlos, had significant attention differences that were resulting in some problems.

While observing in one of his classes, I watched as Carlos left his seat, ran over to a globe in the back of the room, and began spinning it. He smiled from ear to ear as he watched the globe whirl.

"Carlos, where do you need to be?" The teacher's tone was respectful. Carlos complied with the indirect request by returning to his seat, but then two minutes later, he was back at the globe. The teacher sighed and raised her voice a bit. "Carlos! What is your responsibility right now?" He sheepishly returned to his seat.

When Carlos got up for the third time, we realized that the good classroom management the teacher employed was not working. The teacher and I decided to run an experiment. I asked Carlos to tell me what his teacher wanted.

"For me to pay attention and not spin the globe."

"Do you want to do what she wants?"

He nodded vigorously. He knew what his teacher wanted, and he seemed to want the same but was thus far unsuccessful. I then gave Carlos a stress ball, with instructions to try to pay attention and to squeeze the ball instead of running across the room to the globe. I gave the rest of the class the job of observing Carlos to see if he was successful at the following two things:

• staying with the class
• paying attention to the teacher

The teacher continued the lesson, a detailed profile of President Franklin D. Roosevelt. The teacher spoke for about 10 minutes. Carlos's squeezing was intense. He stayed in his chair but seemed to focus all his attention on the stress ball. He never looked up at the teacher and didn't seem to be aware of anything but the ball.

After 10 minutes I interrupted the experiment and asked the class what they saw. "Did Carlos stay with the class?"

They all responded yes.

"Did he pay attention to the teacher?"

In chorus: "Noooo!"

I said, "Let's check that out with Carlos." I asked him if he was successful at his goal to stay with the class.

"Yep." He grinned, never taking his eyes off the ball.

"Were you successful at paying attention to the teacher?"

"Yep." He was beaming. "She was teaching us about President Franklin Roosevelt, and how he brought hope to the people who had gone through the Great Depression. And how he said, 'The only thing we have to fear is fear itself.'"

Carlos went on with more details of the lesson. Although he hadn't looked focused, he could recount almost word for word the content of the lesson. I congratulated him and asked the class again if he was successful at paying attention. They had a different answer that time.

Using a stress ball was a simple modification to help Carlos maintain his focus. That modification restored peace to the classroom and brought joy to the students and teacher alike. Teachers deserve and need training and tips like this to help them interpret and appropriately respond to student behaviors. The exclusive use of traditional methods to enforce compliance typically results only in confusion for the child, disruption of the class, and a frustrating sense of failure for the teacher.

"It's Not Fair to the Rest of the Kids"

Some folks believe fairness is treating everyone the same. At Monarch we believe this definition of fairness is unfair! Real fairness occurs when people get what they need.

Typically siblings of a young person with special needs struggle with their brother's or sister's getting more attention, time, and effort from the parents. Siblings have a hard time accepting that this happens because their brother or sister has greater needs. That principle of serving the greater need is an adult concept that is difficult for some children to understand and must be translated for them.

In a scene from *Star Trek II: The Wrath of Khan* (1982, 113 minutes, rated PG), Mr. Spock chooses to sacrifice his own life by entering a radiation-filled chamber to get the engines back online and save the rest of the crew. As he slowly dies, Spock whispers through the glass to Captain Kirk: "It is logical. The needs of the many outweigh . . ."

" . . . the needs of the few," Kirk replies sadly.

Often young people with special needs are "sacrificed" from classrooms because it is believed their presence will detract from the learning of the other students. This too is logical. If teachers spend all their time dealing with one student, then learning is compromised for the rest of the class.

In situations like this, though, all the time being spent is usually more about the teacher trying to enforce compliance instead of trying to understand how the young people learn best. Ironically a classroom that emphasizes sameness and neglects individualization often ends up with more problems in the long run. It is not the presence of young people with special needs that detracts from the learning of the other students. Instead it is treating everyone the same way that creates chaos. The goals of organization, order, and progress are best reached when teachers allow the students to learn flexibly in the ways that complement their strengths and supplement their weaknesses.

We can all agree that no one needs to be sacrificed for the good of the other learners. With teacher training, modification of the environment, and changes to the curriculum, young people with special needs can thrive where they once were unsuccessful. The great news is that this training and modification will benefit all the students in the classroom.

Ultimately fairness demands we do everything we can to suffer all the children to come, regardless of their differences.

"We Don't Have Any Young People like That in Our Community"

Yes, you do. You have youth with diagnoses and others who have not been diagnosed.

The ones in your program are probably the undiagnosed students with special challenges. In any given group of young people, you are going to find variances in development. Students differ in their readiness to work with a teacher, their ability to pay attention, their emotional maturity, and their skills at relating socially. The diagnosed young people in your community are probably not attending your religious education classes.

If you observe a group of young people in your community, you will see them. You'll see the girl whose head turns at every little noise. You'll see the boy who can't seem to keep his papers organized. There's one who seems sad all the time. And another who doesn't seem to have any friends. They are with you, and the normal religious education classroom structure does not work well for them.

"It's too hard," shared a Monarch parent whose son has autism. "We can't go to church. We tried it for a few weeks, and he would go crawling under the pews, and we'd have to go searching for him in the middle of the service. People didn't understand what we were dealing with. They just thought we were bad parents."

Another parent shared the following about their son, who has Tourette's syndrome: "He went [to church] for a while, but not anymore. We encouraged him and pushed him to go. But his tics got bad, and he was worried he was bothering people. He was uncomfortable, didn't have any friends, and got teased all the time. He felt everybody was being mean to him. Finally he would have a meltdown and refuse to go. I would love for him to be able to go and have a good experience at church."

One of the Monarch fathers commented about his son's Confirmation program: "It's not a good program even for normal kids. It's too disruptive. It's bad because it's too unstructured. Kids are out of control, and that makes it really hard to follow. The lessons go too quickly to follow. It's way too stimulating, with kids yelling out answers to the questions before my son even understands the questions. When I talked to the leaders of the program, they gave me books and workbooks. They suggested that I teach him individually at home."

In response this boy asked his father: "Why is God punishing me? I've been praying and praying, and I don't think there is a God. Why do I have to wake up and be me each day?"

Likely, families in your community have attempted to participate in church programs but, because of difficulties, have opted out. This can occur outside the awareness of youth leaders, giving the false impression that no youth in the community have special needs. But in fact they are out there, and if you build a welcoming, inclusive program, you will see them return.

For the Good of the Community

When young people struggle with these challenges, the last thing in the world they need is rejection from their communities of faith. These young people are not the only ones hurt by this. Exclusion deprives all youth of the challenges and benefits of learning to accept others regardless of their differences and to learn from different perspectives. When the one is sacrificed, the many are also deprived!

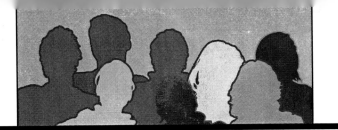

2

The Father Knows Best

A Real-Life Experience

It is not altogether clear whether his neurological differences were genetically based or a result of his traumatic experiences in early childhood. Perhaps it was a combination of both. He was born into abject poverty in a rough, over-populated neighborhood on the outskirts of Memphis, where beatings and murders were common. His mother abandoned him in a rich neighborhood when he was just an infant. She was powerless to protect him and hoped someone would find him and care for him. Thankfully a wealthy family discovered and eventually adopted him.

Throughout his life he exhibited symptoms of impulsivity and aggression, dealing with problems through impulsive acts of violence. This was compounded by severe communication problems. At one point he came upon two men fighting in the street, but instead of calling the police, he jumped into the fight and ended up killing one of the men. When the other ran off, he hauled off the body, buried it, and hoped no one would find out. Later he discovered that a warrant had been issued for his arrest. His fear of the death penalty led him to run away.

While on the run, he continued to act impulsively, but one fight at a local watering hole resulted in a change of luck. One of the women there was impressed by his fighting prowess and asked him to join her for a bite to eat. They hit it off, dated for a while, and ended up getting married. He settled down, had a son, and for a while, it looked like everything was going to be okay.

That's when he started hearing the voices. He was clearly suffering symptoms consistent with schizophrenia. He started hallucinating and developed what could be described as delusions of grandeur. He told his wife that God was speaking to him and had a special mission for him. Struggling to get the words out, he explained that God wanted him to go back to where he had killed the man. God wanted him to threaten the authorities with violence and death.

His wife was overwhelmed by this and feared for his life. She wept as she watched Moses and his brother, Aaron, head out for Egypt.

Examples Throughout the Scriptures

When asked to identify scriptural characters with disabilities, most people will typically mention Job or those cured by Jesus in the New Testament. But if you take a closer look at the main characters in the stories of the Bible, you'll be hard pressed to find a flawless hero.

What you will find is a cast of characters with extraordinary strengths and ordinary human weaknesses. Let's take a look at some of the men and women of the Scriptures who had special needs:

- Noah is diligent and righteous, but one of the first things he does when he gets off the ark is to get drunk (see Genesis 9:21).
- Jacob's role as patriarch continues in spite of a serious hip injury that causes him unrelenting pain (see Genesis 32:25–33).
- Samson is dedicated to God from the day he is born, is blessed with extraordinary strength, and serves as one of the judges (rulers of Israel before the monarchies of Saul, David, Solomon, and the other kings of the Old Testament). Throughout his life Samson has a difficult time regulating his emotions and is prone to impulsive, angry meltdowns (see Judges, chapters 14–16).
- Jesus chooses Simon Peter as his "rock," yet at the same time, Peter is impulsive in his words and actions (see Matthew 16:16–18, 26:33, and 26:69–75).
- Mary Magdalene is stricken with seven demons, yet Christ chooses her to be the first witness to his Resurrection (see Mark 16:9).
- Paul is instrumental in spreading the Good News to the entire known world but has a "thorn of the flesh" (see 2 Corinthians 12:7), a mental and moral struggle he lives with throughout his life.

None of these important figures considered themselves worthy of the significant roles God had in mind for them, and their weaknesses made it hard for them to recognize the value of their contributions. In a way they were right. Alone they could never have fulfilled their important roles. Only through working in community, relying on the help of God and others, could they achieve their goals.

Moses's Story

Moses felt unworthy when God called him. He tried to opt out of his special role in the community. He couldn't imagine having the ability to express himself and influence others in the way God deserved. Certainly an understandable response considering the mission Moses was being asked to fulfill! This is similar to the opting out that occurs with so many of our families who have youth with special needs. It is equally understandable considering how challenging it can be for these youth to be successful in environments that do not support them. Like Moses these youth feel inadequate to the task. But in the same way God provides support for Moses, we can provide support for our youth with special needs in our religious education and youth ministry programs.

Feeling inadequate and recognizing and owning his weaknesses, Moses humbly asked that God reconsider his request: "O my Lord, I have never been eloquent, neither in the past nor even now that you have spoken to your servant; but I am slow of speech and slow of tongue" (Exodus 4:10).

God promised to give Moses the words to say and to help him with his speech. Moses still insisted that God send someone else. The scriptural account of God's response to Moses is simply delightful. What would you expect from God at this point in the story? gentle encouragement? Possibly something like: "Everything's going this to be okay, Moses. So you're not the best speaker in the world? So what? You're the best you in the world! You can do it, man! Now, come give me a hug . . ."

Maybe a little divine cajoling, like this: "You know I could have picked Aaron for the role. I mean, I think he wanted the gig. But Mo, baby, Aaron lacks your . . . panache. You've got a certain 'Chuck Heston' dramatic quality that recommends you for the job. So come on, whad'ya say?"

Or perhaps a more empathetic approach along these lines: "Moses, you're not the only one who has trouble speaking. Look at me; I talked to you through a burning bush, for crying out loud! One time, I had to give a talk to the heavenly host about the new creatures of the earth, and I looked down and realized I'd left my notes back at the ranch. (Heaven, of course, is somewhere in the Texas Hill Country!) I was sweating, and my hands were shaking, and I just started making stuff up, and that's why we now have the platypus, seahorses, giraffes, and armadillos . . ."

No, the author of the Book of Exodus describes God's response not as one of sympathy, coaxing, or understanding. It is characterized by anger (see Exodus 4:14). It is the deepest of rumbling frustration that is so often attributed to God when we show a lack of trust in providential care. Remember these classic scriptural moments of human doubt:

"I heard the sound of you in the garden, and I was afraid, because I was naked; and I hid myself" (Genesis 3:10). *rumble*

"Why did you bring us out of Egypt, to kill us and our children and livestock with thirst?"(Genesis 17:3). *grrr*

"Lord, if you had been here, my brother would not have died" (John 11:21). *snort*

This divine anger is a reaction to the dismissal of the covenantal character of God's relationship with humans. When Moses and others in the Scriptures communicate doubt in response to God's call, they are saying: "You know that part of the Covenant: 'I will be your God'? Well, God, I just don't trust it."

In anger God reminds Moses that God is the architect of all creation, which includes the creation of Moses—just as he is, communication problems and all. Moses is called not in spite of his weaknesses but as a whole person, complete with weaknesses and strengths. In the same way, people of faith are called wholly to full participation in their faith communities. The part so often missed is that individuals don't respond to God's call alone. "Yes, we will do it," is much easier to say than, "Yes, I will do it." If you read the stories of those in the Scriptures whom God calls, you will discover that God not only provides direct support but also supplies a cast of supporting actors who help God's Chosen People achieve their goals.

In the story of Moses, that support is both figurative and literal. When facing the Pharaoh, Aaron speaks for Moses, providing an accommodation for Moses's communication difficulties. God inspires Moses, then Moses tells Aaron what to say, and then Aaron acts as Moses's spokesman in public. It's clearly a team effort. (see Exodus 7:1–2).

The literal support is illustrated in the following account of the battle with the Amalekites:

Then Amalek came and fought with Israel at Rephidim. Moses said to Joshua, "Choose some men for us and go out; fight with Amalek. Tomorrow I will stand on the top of the hill with the staff of God in my hand." So Joshua did as Moses told him, and fought with Amalek, while Moses, Aaron, and Hur went up to the top of the hill. Whenever Moses held up his hand, Israel prevailed; and whenever he lowered his hand, Amalek prevailed. But Moses' hands grew weary; so they took a stone and put it under him, and he sat on it. Aaron and Hur held up his hands, one on one side, and the other on the other side; so his hands were steady until the sun set. (Exodus 17:8–12)

Who are the Aarons and Hurs in your life? Who supports you when you are tired? Whom do you support in this way? Think about how your story would be different without these relationships. When fear and doubt lead us to say no to God's call, consider how we are isolating ourselves from the potential support of family, friends, and community. Separation and isolation rob us of our ability and our hope. Joining with family and community, as Moses did with Aaron and Hur, gives us strength and courage.

This is a wonderful scriptural story for many reasons. One life lesson it teaches is that all of us, no matter how great, need support sometimes. None of us is immune from one day acquiring, through illness or accident, a special need similar to those of people who are excluded.

We Are All Vulnerable

In one of the Jewish commentaries of Exodus is a delightful story in which Moses, as a toddler, grabs the crown from the Pharaoh's head and places it on his own. The Pharaoh's advisors worry that Moses may have done it deliberately and knowingly, as a sign of his desire to usurp the throne.

Pharaoh sends for all the wise men of Egypt to advise him in this matter. The Angel Gabriel, disguised as a wise man, proposes that an onyx stone and a coal of fire be placed before Moses. If the boy chooses the onyx stone, then the Pharaoh will know Moses has wisdom enough to have deliberately taken the crown, and that he should be killed. If Moses chooses the hot coal, then Pharaoh will know the boy is blameless in his taking of the crown. Pharaoh agrees to this test, and when the onyx stone and coal of fire are placed before Moses, his hand is secretly guided by the angel to the coal. Moses grabs the coal and places it in his mouth, and his lips and tongue are burned. This results not only in the Pharaoh's sparing of Moses's life but also in Moses's thereafter stuttering and speaking slowly (adapted from Rabbi Ephraim Buchwald, "The Making of a Concerned Jewish Leader").

This story is a good reminder that we are all vulnerable to events that may disable us in some way, but also that in some mysterious way, God may use these disabilities for the greater good. It is not reasonable to believe God deliberately inflicts suffering, but many believe and have witnessed God's hand in bringing much good from affliction or disability. In supporting Moses, Aaron and Hur also benefit, as do all the Israelites.

Our Experiences at The Monarch School

In the same way as Moses, Aaron, Hur, and the Israelites, we at The Monarch School support our students, and we also learn from and grow with them. It's important to point out, though, that Monarch students retain ownership of their growth and learning. Aaron and Hur do not replace Moses, nor do they carry him. Moses still owns the role of leader in the battle.

Sadly youth with special needs are often robbed of the ownership of their own development. The desire to help can lead adults to provide too much replacement help ("I'll do it for you"). The result is that the youth are carried instead of supported. They then get stuck and become overly dependent on the adults around them.

Lives are changed at The Monarch School, not through the efforts of any one individual but rather through the combined work of a team of Aarons and Hurs committed to working together to support the youth in their struggles to grow. The youth at Monarch, to the degree they are able, retain ownership of their development. They set goals, reflect on their progress, and build plans for success. Like Aaron and Hur, Monarch staff members support the youth when they need it, but we do not carry them. In the same way, all youth in religious education and youth ministry programs, to the degree they are able, should maintain ownership of their religious understandings and spiritual growth.

One of the saddest scenes is when families of youth with special needs opt out of participating in faith communities because they don't feel enough support for their young people to be successful. For example, those who have Tourette's syndrome are often not welcome in worship gatherings due to the disruption their verbalizations cause. They may hoot or call out words, and many people find this distracting. But consider all the ambient noises that are just as loud as a Tourette's vocalization but that are perfectly acceptable to the community. A hearty cough or sneeze is often the same volume or more than a Tourette's verbalization, and there is a veritable chorus of coughs through-out most congregational gatherings. The only reason Tourette's vocalizations disrupt is because they are unusual.

If the members of the community have the compassion to open their arms to embrace those with this syndrome, they will notice that the vocalizations soon become ambient and blend in with the cacophony of coughs, throat clearing, sneezes, and other noises always present in large gatherings of people.

When there is no acceptance in the community, the families of these people withdraw, and the community is silent in response. We at The Monarch School have heard the same story from many different parents—they tried it, it didn't work, they stopped attending. End of story.

When parents tell us their youth are no longer involved in religious education programs, we always ask them, "When you stopped attending, did anyone call to ask why or to invite you back?"

We Are Called to Respond Differently

You are encouraged to respond to the Great Commission (see Matthew 28:18–20) by creating that yes in your community. Please respond passionately when community members are marginalized. When a youth with special needs stops participating, and the teacher or ministry leader is relieved because the "disruption" or her or his own anxiety has ended, please say: "No. She is one of us. Let's invite her back, and let's provide the support she needs to be successfully present."

The last clause is crucial. If the community is not prepared to modify its environment, curriculum, and hearts to accommodate a young person with special needs, then it just isn't going to work. Welcoming someone into a setting in which she or he will fail is not welcoming at all. The Aarons and Hurs need to be in place, ready to support a youth with special needs in her or his struggles.

Transforming Hearts

The good news is that the modifications to the environment and the curriculum are not difficult to implement. Much harder is the work of transforming hearts to accept and undertake the efforts.

You may encounter people in your community who reject, either philosophically or practically, your efforts to transform religious education programs to be more inclusive. Following are a few fictitious examples of people you might encounter:

The Host of the Book
Readers, I'd like to introduce you to David Dubious.

David
Hello. How are you doing?

The Host
Just great, David, and welcome to chapter 2 of A Place for All: Ministry for Youth with Special Needs.

David
So you're writing a book about mythology?

The Host
No, why would you say that?

David
Because I heard you say "special needs."

The Host
So, you don't believe some children have special needs?

David
Well, if a kid's in a wheelchair, I'll be the first one
up here on a Saturday to build him a ramp. But if you
start talking about attention deficit disorder (ADD),
obsessive-compulsive disorder (OCD), and other
psychobabble, then no, I don't believe it.

The Host
But David, research shows that these children's
neurological differences cause significant difficulties
when they try to function in ordinary classrooms.
They have trouble focusing, staying on task, regulating
their emotions . . .

David
Yes, and that neurological research is flawed. ADD
is society's new label for what we used to call lazy
or undisciplined.

The Host
Thanks for sharing your perspective, David.
Ladies and gentlemen, please give a warm welcome
to our next guest, Polly Pragmatic.

Polly
Thank you for inviting me into your book. I think
what you're advocating is fantastic!

The Host
That's wonderful, Polly. So you don't agree with David's
assessment of special needs youth?

Polly
Oh, heavens, no. Our family has several children
with attention deficit-hyperactivity disorder (ADHD).
I know it's real, and I know meds and modifications
are necessary for our kids. We have a neighbor boy
with Tourette's syndrome too. I know he can't help it
when he has those tics.

The Host
Well, it's nice to hear you have a good understanding
of these neurological differences. So will you be using

the book to make some changes in your parish's religious
education and youth ministry programs?

Polly
I'm afraid not. It just wouldn't be possible
in our community.

The Host
Why not?

Polly
Well, first of all, our church budget is tight,
so we don't have a lot of money to spend on teacher
training and classroom modifications. Second, all our
Sunday school teachers are volunteers, not professional
teachers. They haven't been trained to deal with normal
young people, much less youth with special needs.
And even if we got somebody to train the teachers and
volunteers, half of them would quit rather than spend
extra time attending the training classes. We have
a hard time finding enough volunteers as it is. I know
it's important, and it breaks my heart to have those
poor kids left out, but . . .

The Host
So you understand the need, but you're not willing to
work to make it happen?

Polly
I care about these kids; really I do . . . but at our
church, it just wouldn't work.

The Host
If others at your church also believe as you do, Polly,
then you're probably right.

Why do so many in ministry have such a fear of working with and for
young people with special needs? What in our culture leads us to choose not
to be inviting to children with disabilities, differences, and quirks?

Based on our experiences at The Monarch School, we have found that
some people are afraid. They may be afraid of contagion—that somehow
other students will begin acquiring these characteristics. They may be afraid of
the unusual in favor of "normality." Unfortunately this fear can result in the
loss of the opportunity to gain a broader appreciation of the richness of our
lives by including those who have not only special needs for themselves but
also special gifts of perspective for all of us.

Having a David or a Polly can be discouraging, but please don't let them shut you down as you work with others to transform your communities. As a ministry leader, your work should include providing religious education and youth ministry programs with appropriate modifications so the efforts of the parish to educate and minister include all young people. This book will show you ways to do that. Trust that God will provide the transformative power to the Davids and Pollys in your communities, through the Word and the Spirit. The Scriptures make us aware that even the greatest of us has considerable weaknesses, and they assure us that God loves us without conditions. God's call does not depend on our perfection, just our persistence and trust. God calls us, loves us, and accepts us as we are.

The Spirit provides us with the ability to see others through the eyes of God. All are created in the divine image—regardless of physical, mental, or emotional differences. All equally deserve God's love. All are welcome in the Reign of God. We must ask ourselves, "Do our faith communities, religious education classrooms, and youth ministry programs reflect God's unconditional acceptance of all of us?"

3

A Different Take

"Billy Goes to Confirmation Class, Take One"

"Quiet on the set! Speed! And . . . action!"

Fade-in: A lanky boy, BILLY, in his early teens shuffles down the sidewalk, shoulders hunched in tension. Beside him walks MOTHER, a middle-aged woman, looking concerned.

Mother
Are you sure you don't want me to come with you, Billy?

Billy
(He glares at her and breathes deeply and loudly through his nostrils as he gathers his thoughts.)
No.

(He speaks quietly, but his furrowed brow and hostile tone make clear his anger and annoyance.)
I don't want you to come with me.

(Billy glances up at several youth getting dropped off and entering the building unescorted.)
The first meeting is for kids only.

Mother
(with hesitation)
Okay, honey; I hope it goes well.
I'll be in the car if you need me.

Billy

(Without responding to his mother, he continues down the walkway and shuffles slowly into the room, his eyes on his feet. The room is brightly lit, and groups of teens fill the room with laughter and conversation.

(He grabs the first seat he can find. The conversations get louder and louder as more students enter. Close-up on Billy as he clutches the sides of his chair and begins to rock back and forth. He shields his eyes from the bright fluorescent lighting, his eyes pressed tightly shut.

(A girl close by laughs loudly in response to an unheard comment from another girl. Billy reacts as if she were shrieking at him. He puts his hands over his ears and continues to rock in his chair, but faster and with an expression of pain building. Others do not notice this behavior.

(Quick zoom on Billy as he abruptly stands, picks up the chair, and throws it to the floor. He raises his fists in the air.)

SHUUUUUT UUUUUUUP!

(The room becomes immediately silent as all eyes turn toward Billy.)

"Cut!"

Please take a few moments to complete the preceding scene in your imagination, using the following reflection questions:

- How do the youth respond to Billy's outburst?
- How do the adults in the room respond?
- How do they judge Billy's behavior?
- How are they likely to react?
- What effect will their reactions have on Billy?
- How will Billy respond to them?

Do your answers to these questions include judgmental or rude comments from teens? Perhaps you complete the scene with the youth saying things like, "What is his problem?" or "That dude is going postal!" Without understanding the causes of disruptive behavior, teens can be unknowingly cruel in their judgments and reactions. When they are aware, however, they can also be incredibly understanding and supportive.

Without awareness adults also can misinterpret and respond to special needs issues as if they were willful disruptions on the part of the youth. In the previous scene, Billy's actions are disruptive, but his intention is not to be rebellious or oppositional. He is communicating to the community that he is overwhelmed. He is "teaching" the community that he can't handle the sensory input around him.

Typical disciplinary approaches communicate standards and expectations and then enforce these standards through consequences for infractions. These consequences can include temporary or permanent exclusion from the community, loss of privileges, and issuing of apologies. All these consequences are designed to encourage compliance, but using these approaches in situations like Billy's is ineffective at best, and at worst, increases the intensity of the disruptive behavior.

Most people at some time have the experience of witnessing a temper tantrum of a child in a grocery store, with a parent close by, trying to help the child get under control. Think about your reaction when you witness this. Are you curious? Do you ask yourself: "I wonder why this child is screaming and thrashing around on the floor? Does the child have a neurological difference that makes it difficult to regulate emotions?" Are you judging? Maybe you say to yourself, "That kid is a total brat" or "That inept parent needs to get control over that kid."

The latter responses are more likely, and it's not difficult to understand why. Consider how misbehavior was handled when you were a child. Most of us grew up in homes and schools where authority figures responded to this kind of behavior with a strong correction like "Stop that right now!" or a threat like: "If you don't stop that . . ." The notion of substituting curiosity as a response would have been seen as coddling or weak: "What's going on, sweetheart?"

But by substituting curiosity ("I wonder what caused Billy to scream and throw the chair?") for judgment ("Billy is misbehaving"), we are better able to get to the root of the issue in a problem-solving mode rather than a punitive enforcement mode. When an entire community addresses all behavior issues this way and prepares proactively to deal with them, the results are astounding.

"Billy Goes to Confirmation Class, Take Two"

"Quiet on the set! Speed! "And . . . action!"

Fade-in: Three people are sitting in a meeting room with conversation already in progress. The DIRECTOR OF

RELIGIOUS EDUCATION (DRE) sits at the head of the table, with CATECHIST 1 and CATECHIST 2 on either side. All have binders open, and the catechists are taking notes.

DRE

(in midsentence)

. . . with Asperger's syndrome have a fascination and expertise with unusual or narrow areas of interest. So if we each take a few minutes to do an Internet search on different models of trains, it will give us some conversation starters with Jeremy.

Catechist 1

(smiling)

How fun. Okay, will do.

DRE

We have one more student to discuss. His name is Billy. In the special needs section of his registration form, Billy's mom tells us he has sensory integration issues.

Catechist 2

I remember that from the catechist special needs training. So he has problems processing information he receives through his senses, like touch or movement.

Catechist 1

And it could be over- or underreaction to things he sees and feels, right?

DRE

That's right. In Billy's case, he is very sensitive to bright lights.

Catechist 1

I can understand that. I hate those bright fluorescent lights myself!

Catechist 2

We've got that covered with the dim section of the room.

DRE

Let's make sure the dim section is at the entrance so he doesn't have to deal with the jarring experience of the bright lights on his way to the dimmer part of the room.

Catechist 1
What about using the tinted lenses?

DRE
(referring to binder)
We have three others who will be using them, so he
might feel comfortable. But on his form, his mother
shared that he is especially sensitive to being singled
out. He wants to look like all the other kids.

Catechist 1
Why don't we just make them available to him
and let him decide?

DRE
Good plan. And we'll also need to have the
noise-reduction headphones available.

Catechist 2
So Billy is hypersensitive to loud noises?

DRE
Very. Mom says he is (reading) "quickly and easily
overwhelmed in loud environments."

Catechist 2
Well, it's going to be really loud as kids enter . . .

Catechist 1
And he might feel embarrassed to wear
the headphones . . .

Catechist 2
But after the pastor's talk on inclusion, I don't think
the other kids will make fun of him.

Catechist 1
Probably not, but he still might feel embarrassed.

DRE
What if we set up the snacks and drinks in small
meeting rooms right off the hall? That would provide
a quieter area that's still connected to the hall.

Catechist 2
Good idea.

Catechist 1
Great. Then he can choose for himself how he deals
with the noise level.

DRE
Okay, good. Now let's talk about the room setup.

"Cut!"

Again, take a few moments to reflect. Imagine how Billy's experience at his first Confirmation class would be different as a result of the previous scene. Consider how a little attention and preparation (care and love) can make a huge difference not just in the initial experience but also in the likelihood of youth like Billy ever being accepted in and connected to the community.

Without this preparation the first scene can end up being the end of the screenplay. Without advanced knowledge and preparation, the adult leaders would probably approach this from a strict disciplinary perspective. Using this approach would most likely result in Billy's being sent home that evening. At home the lights can be dimmed, Mom is understanding, and Billy feels safe and isn't made fun of. With the same overwhelming stimuli waiting for him, along with a reputation of troublemaker and an expectation to control his emotions in the midst of this overwhelming environment, why in the world would Billy have any motivation to return to Confirmation class?

Youth like Billy often end up permanently outside the faith community, living the rest of their already-challenged lives disconnected from what could be a sustaining and transformative support system for them. The following is an overview of the steps toward building this support system in your communities. I will use the metaphor of farming to help explain each step. Just as in farming, these steps take time and preparation before you see the benefits of your hard work. Later chapters will specifically address and expand on each of the following steps.

1. Learning How to Farm

If you plan to serve with others as the catalyst for change in the community, you must have a good understanding of the special needs of the youth you are likely to encounter. It is not essential that you become an expert in special education, but you should know the basics and develop an openness and flexibility to differences in youth.

In addition, a critical part of your preparation is developing an awareness of what life is like for families of children with special needs. Understanding the demands and difficulties will motivate you to provide an environment that gives them a respite from their struggles. Ahead you'll find good, fundamental information and insights, as well as recommendations for other expert sources.

2. Preparing the Soil

Shared understanding and commitment are essential to the success of a program that seeks to be truly inclusive. Garnering the support and participation of staff, as well as other members of the church, will ensure a spirit of welcoming not only in the program you work with but also in the entire community. You cannot do this alone. You must join with, and have the support of other equally curious educators. To help you prepare the soil, this book includes sample talks, announcements, and strategies to raise awareness and promote support for the program.

With guidance from a special education professional, you'll also want to modify your environment and curriculum to provide accommodations and interventions for the many learning differences and styles you will encounter in the youth who attend. This book provides examples of environments and lesson plans that have been modified to be more inclusive. Also included are sample registration forms that sensitively solicit information about special needs.

3. Gathering and Training the Workers

You must surround yourself with a team of people devoted to sharing this adventure with you. Include staff, as well as volunteers, and seek out people in the community who have knowledge and expertise in special education to facilitate training sessions for all who will work in the program. Together this team will develop a vision statement and a specific plan for building a more welcoming and inclusive community. Included are guidelines for building your team and a sample lesson plan from a Monarch School training for religious educators.

4. Sowing the Seeds

How exciting it will be, after all this preparation, to open your doors to include more youth than ever before! Even though much can be done in advance, the real work begins when the youth walk through the door. The registration information is only a first step. Every young person is unique, and your strategies will not be "one size fits all." Even within specific diagnoses are huge variations in functioning. One student with autism may be able to function with little or no accommodation, whereas another with the same diagnosis may require numerous modifications to be successful.

We learn the most about the individual needs of each student from being in relationship with each of them. They will teach you how they learn best and what their needs are. You and your teachers will serve as coaches for the youth, helping them take ownership of their own challenges.

5. Nourishing the Crops

As your community grows in welcoming youth with special needs, constant care is essential. Each day will not be full sun with a brief but thorough afternoon shower. You may have days like these, but you may also have days of drought, in which the students seem to be withering in spite of your care, or days of thunderstorms, during which the youth may experience emotional upset. On these days remind yourself that it is not just your preparation, skills, and intentions that determine how a class day will proceed. Mood, energy levels, circumstances at home, and variations in student readiness, along with many other factors, will combine with your preparation and openness to create a community that sometimes gets it right and sometimes doesn't. The goal is not to perfect the environment but rather to make it a safe place to not get it perfect every time, a safe place to practice.

As every community does, you will experience problems, breakdowns in communication, and conflicts. Your job is not to try to eliminate these occurrences, because they are inevitable in every community, but instead to instill practices and traditions of dealing with these issues in ways that help youth feel safe and lead them toward reconciliation, forgiveness, and bearing with one another gently. Ahead you'll read about how these practices are implemented at The Monarch School and how you can integrate them into your community.

6. Reaping the Harvest

Ultimately you and your team will rejoice in the experience of a truly welcoming and inclusive community and will delight in the transformative power that open arms and open doors can bring.

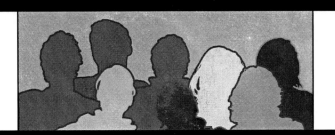

4

Learning How to Farm

Although it is not necessary for you to become an expert in special education to be more welcoming to youth with special needs, it will be helpful for you to have a basic understanding of the various challenges you may see in the youth you serve. Although this book does not provide an exhaustive list of special needs diagnoses, it does provide basic information about those you are most likely to encounter.

Attention Differences

Roses are red,
violets are blue,
I have attention deficit disorder,
and . . . (*looks to the side, pointing*) ooh, shiny!

When one of our students shared this poem, we were delighted he could joke about his distractibility. For many of our youth, however, attention differences are not a laughing matter; they can be debilitating.

Attention differences such as the inability to maintain focus, high levels of distractibility, and impulsivity can severely impair a student's ability to learn. If that weren't difficult enough, many students with attention differences also have to cope with a lack of acceptance or support from teachers, parents, and peers. The problem occurs when the symptoms of ADD or ADHD are misinterpreted as willful. Hyperactivity becomes "won't sit still." Distractibility is described as "refuses to pay attention." Youth who are impulsive are called "irresponsible" or "reckless."

This misinterpretation or mischaracterization of attention differences as a matter of choice is unfortunate but not surprising. If a wheelchair-bound student were described as "refuses to walk," that would be surprising. But because some of the milder symptoms of ADD and ADHD are shared at some time by almost all of us, it is easy to label these behaviors as "willful."

The following are the symptoms of ADD or ADHD as described in the *Diagnostic and Statistical Manual of Mental Disorders,* fourth edition:

Inattention
- Often does not give close attention to details or makes careless mistakes in schoolwork, work, or other activities.
- Often has trouble keeping attention on tasks or play activities.
- Often does not seem to listen when spoken to directly.
- Often does not follow instructions and fails to finish schoolwork, chores, or duties in the workplace (not due to oppositional behavior or failure to understand instructions).
- Often has trouble organizing activities.
- Often avoids, dislikes, or doesn't want to do things that take a lot of mental effort for a long period of time (such as schoolwork or homework).
- Often loses things needed for tasks and activities (such as toys, school assignments, pencils, books, or tools).
- Is often easily distracted.
- Is often forgetful in daily activities.

Hyperactivity
- Often fidgets with hands or feet or squirms in seat.
- Often gets up from seat when remaining in seat is expected.
- Often runs about or climbs when and where it is not appropriate (adolescents or adults may feel very restless).
- Often has trouble playing or enjoying leisure activities quietly.
- Is often on the go or often acts as if driven by a motor.
- Often talks excessively.

Impulsivity
- Often blurts out answers before questions have been finished.
- Often has trouble waiting one's turn.
- Often interrupts or intrudes on others (e.g., butts into conversations or games).

(Page 92)

Please read through the symptoms, checking off those that describe you and your behavior at one time or another. People typically exhibit most of these behaviors at some point in their lives, depending on the contexts and circumstances. For this reason some people have difficulty accepting these behaviors as evidence of a disability or disorder. Rather than get bogged down in trying to decide whether a behavior is willful or neurological in origin, pragmatic teachers approach all attention differences with the same toolbox of strategies, accommodations, and interventions, problem-solving with the youth to help them take ownership of their struggles and ultimately be more successful.

As with most disabilities, attention differences vary from mild to severe. Virtually every group of youth includes some with attention differences that affect their learning in some way.

Autism

Young people with autism typically have developmental differences in their social interactions, communications, and abilities to engage in symbolic or imaginative play. But the label "autistic" can cover behaviors that range from a nonverbal child who is completely shut off from the rest of the world to a very high-functioning adult, living independently and considered by others to be only quirky.

Add to this the misunderstandings resulting from Hollywood portrayals of autism, and it is easy to understand why many people are confused about what autism really is. When thinking about autism, most people consider the 1988 Academy Award–winning film *Rain Man* (128 minutes, rated R). In the film Dustin Hoffman portrays a man, Raymond, who has autism, as well as savant syndrome. The characteristics of this second, extremely rare, condition include heightened memory and extraordinary ability in a specific area, such as mathematics, music, or memorization of trivia. Raymond demonstrates heightened memory skills in his ability to remember entries in a phone book, to recall baseball statistics, and to count cards in Las Vegas.

These abilities can be amazing. One of the students who attended Monarch several years ago could tell you the day of the week your birthday fell on in virtually any year you named! He could also quickly tell you the square root of any number without any hesitation.

Dr. Neal Sarahan, one of our program directors at Monarch, explains these phenomena as follows:

> What happens sometimes to people with autism who have lots of cognitive capacity is that their energy gets focused on idiosyncratic mental processes. Without the benefit of a connection to the social world of shared knowledge, the person still has lots of dedicated cognitive capacity— typically stored in very strong memory functions. And because there is lots of energy, and mental power, their skills can be quite profound, but also most times totally, sadly useless.

In other words the same mental energy that typical people expend on complex interactions in the real world become, in people with savant syndrome, hyperfocused on other areas, resulting in extraordinary skills and talents. Despite these amazing skills and talents, those with savant syndrome often struggle with the simplest relationship skills. Although it contained a sensitive portrayal of autism, *Rain Man* resulted in many people mistakenly assuming that all people with autism have savant abilities. The reality is that most people with autism do not have these extraordinary abilities.

Autism is a spectrum disorder. This means it manifests a range of symptoms from mild to severe. All disorders within the autistic spectrum are referred to as autistic spectrum disorders (ASD) and are also referred to as pervasive developmental disorders (PDD). The labels "autism" or "autistic," as well as "PDD," apply to all individuals whose diagnoses fall in the autistic spectrum.

The labels associated with autism can be quite confusing. The rest of the chapter explains a simple breakdown of the terminology currently used in the DSM-IV and in the mental health community to describe individuals with autism.

The DSM-IV includes the diagnoses of five pervasive developmental disorders, or diagnoses within the autistic spectrum, two of which are very rare. The following paragraphs summarize the three most common diagnoses in the autistic spectrum.

Autistic Disorder

Autistic disorder is a severe form of autism that includes serious impairment in social interaction, language, the ability to engage in symbolic or imaginative play, or any combination of these impairments. Youth with autistic disorder may be nonverbal or have limited verbal expression, sometimes only repeating the words and sounds they hear (echolalia). They show little interest in interacting with others, preferring to be in their own world. Young people with autistic disorder typically engage in repetitive movements, or stimming. Stimming can include the flapping of hands or rocking back and forth. Deficits in cognitive functioning are also commonly present.

Pervasive Developmental Disorder—Not Otherwise Specified (PDD-NOS)

Pervasive developmental disorder is not itself a diagnosis but rather an umbrella term that includes the five diagnoses described in this section. PDD-NOS, often mistakenly described as simply PDD, is a developmental disorder with significant social and communication impairment but in which cognitive and language skills are less impaired than in autistic disorder. Also referred to as atypical autism, the diagnosis PDD-NOS is given to individuals who have autistic characteristics but don't fit the diagnostic criteria of the other PDD diagnoses. Youth with PDD-NOS are also less likely to have repetitive movements than with other ASD diagnoses.

Asperger's Syndrome

Individuals diagnosed with Asperger's syndrome typically have advanced cognitive and language skills but have difficulty forming and maintaining relationships, translating subtle social cues, and expanding beyond a limited range of interests.

Because of their highly developed vocabulary and other language skills, individuals with Asperger's syndrome are often not recognized as having a neurological difference but instead are judged as odd or quirky. They are seen as being highly intelligent but socially awkward. Youth with Asperger's syndrome are often the targets of bullies because of their awkwardness.

Obsessive or narrow interests in unusual topics make conversation challenging for those with Asperger's syndrome. They may want to talk about only one or two topics that interest them and quickly grow bored with conversations about anything else. They also typically are more interested in telling than in back-and-forth, two-way communication. In this mode they can be quite articulate. But in conversations about other topics, and especially in small talk, the conversation is typically awkward, halting, and uncomfortable for them.

Tourette's Syndrome

Of all of the neurological differences, Tourette's syndrome presents one of the greatest challenges for faith communities, as well as for individuals with Tourette's.

People with Tourette's syndrome experience tics, or involuntary vocalizations and body movements. Vocalizations vary with each individual and can include grunts, sniffs, throat clearing, and calling out of words. Typical physical tics include eye twitching, shrugging, head turning, and facial grimacing.

In addition, it is common for those diagnosed with Tourette's also to carry a diagnosis of obsessive-compulsive disorder (described in the next section).

Difficulties often result from the many widely held myths about Tourette's syndrome, which increase fear and anxiety regarding the inclusion of those with the disorder. Some of those myths follow:

Myth 1: All people with Tourette's yell out obscene words and phrases.
Truth: Although a small percentage of people with Tourette's has an uncontrollable use of obscene or offensive language (coprolalia), most do not.

Myth 2: People with Tourette's can control their tics.
Truth: Although tics can be suppressed for a period of time, ultimately they will come out. Similar to holding one's breath, people with Tourette's can control their tics for only brief periods of time.

Myth 3: People with Tourette's cannot live normal lives.
Truth: Although the symptoms of Tourette's can be challenging, and in some cases debilitating, many people with Tourette's live normal lives. It is often the acceptance or rejection of their communities that makes the difference.

Obsessive-Compulsive Disorder (OCD)

Someone with OCD (an anxiety disorder) struggles with obsessions and compulsions. Obsessions are upsetting thoughts and images that come into the person's mind. These thoughts are unwanted and involuntary and result in compulsions, which are actions intended to neutralize the obsessions. The obsessions typically do not involve serious real-life concerns, such as "If I walk down this dark alley, I may get mugged." They are more likely to be relatively trivial, such as "If I step on the cracks in the sidewalk, something horrible will happen," or "I have to turn the lights on and off exactly seven times or my day will be ruined."

These obsessions and compulsions are irrational, and most people with OCD are aware of this. But they feel powerless to ignore the obsessive thoughts, and they experience extreme anxiety unless they complete the compulsive actions. Unlike people with addictions, people with OCD don't experience pleasure when they act out their compulsive tasks.

Young people with OCD who are in religious education settings are especially vulnerable to obsessive feelings of scrupulosity and shame. Obsessions can include exaggerated desires to be perfect, feeling dirty or sinful, or being obsessively afraid of impure thoughts. Obviously it is neither desirable nor practical to avoid topics of morality, conscience, and so on, but teachers and youth ministers can be sensitive to, and aware that, these topics can tap into these extreme, obsessive thoughts in young people with OCD.

Another common feature of OCD is a phobic concern about germs and cleanliness. Fear of contamination may lead to a resistance to touch, sit, or use objects others have used. Be sensitive to these concerns when planning experiences in which youth are expected to touch one another, such as holding hands in a prayer circle.

Typical compulsive acts you may see in your classrooms or youth groups from youth with OCD include the following:
- frequent, repeated, or lengthy hand washing
- specific ways to organize or count movements or objects (such as a strong need for symmetrical balance in artwork, desktop organization, and so forth)

- resistance to touching others
- avoidance of, or discomfort with, certain numbers or symbols
- exaggerated concern for perfection of a completed task

The driving force in the life of a person with OCD is the extreme anxiety that results from obsessive thoughts. The youth in your program who have this condition must be allowed adaptive strategies to alleviate this anxiety—as long as adapting doesn't put them or others at risk. Without this freedom the anxiety can progress to unbearable levels, resulting in severe emotional upset and panic attacks.

Mood Disorders

Disorders affecting mood are much more easily identified in adults than in young people. For example, adults who suffer from depression generally experience sadness, fatigue, and lack of interest in things around them. Youth may also experience these symptoms, but depression in young people can also manifest itself as irritability or anger. Other symptoms may include restlessness, lethargy, and social withdrawal.

Diagnoses of bipolar disorder have significantly increased for young people in the last decade. This condition, formerly referred to as manic-depressive disorder, is a mood disorder characterized by episodes of depression followed by manic episodes of elation and excitability. Depending on where the youth is in the cycle, she or he may appear down in the dumps one day and on top of the world the next.

These mood changes are difficult for peers, especially in youth ministry contexts. Peers may try to cheer up the youth who is depressed. Then when a manic episode appears, it is incorrectly interpreted that the youth feels better. When the youth and adults understand that the mood shifts are more likely a function of neurological wiring than responses to environmental factors, the relationships can occur with much less confusion and frustration.

Eating Disorders

Sadly our culture's narrowly defined concept of "thin is beautiful" has resulted in the emergence of the destructive and sometimes fatal eating disorders anorexia nervosa and bulimia nervosa. Those with anorexia experience an intense fear of gaining weight or becoming fat, thus resorting to a variety of methods to maintain a desired low body weight. This disorder can include binging and purging—extreme overeating followed by forced vomiting or the use of laxatives or diuretics to rid the body of the food. Bulimia is characterized by binge eating, most often followed by purging. Binge eaters eat large amounts of food because they feel no control over their eating.

These disorders occur primarily in females. Early studies estimated that males account for 10 percent of the cases, but a recent study at Harvard University in Cambridge, Massachusetts, revealed that 25 percent of people with anorexia or bulimia, and 40 percent of binge eaters, are men. Both anorexia and bulimia are the results of disturbances in how people perceive their body shape and weight. They see themselves as fat and overweight, in spite of the reality that they are extremely thin and underweight.

Both disorders severely affect an individual's self-esteem. Great care and sensitivity should be taken when discussing the disorders with parents and teens. Because of the serious physical dangers of the disorders, catechists and youth leaders who see signs of them should immediately share their concerns with the parents and urge them to seek help for their son or daughter. Medical doctors or professional counselors often have more specific training to help these parents.

Trichotillomania

Individuals with trichotillomania pull hairs from all parts of their bodies, resulting in significant loss of hair. The most common areas are the scalp, the eyebrows, and the eyelashes. Those with the disorder experience pleasure when pulling out their hair and feel tense when they try to resist the urge. The hair pulling can also include playing with, examining, or in some cases, consuming the hair.

Clearly this behavior can result in social challenges for young people. As with many other neurological issues, making others aware is the first step toward acceptance and compassion. Peers who are aware of and understand the disorder are much more likely to be supportive and accepting of someone with it.

Unique in the Universe

The use of diagnostic information is helpful in identifying and treating young people with neurological differences. However, a young person is not a diagnosis. Knowing a young person's diagnosis is a good starting point, but it doesn't take the place of getting to know her or him as an individual. As with typical youth, no two young people with autism are alike. Yes, tics are common for everyone with Tourette's, but there is tremendous variation in the effect tics have. Youth with depression may or may not look sad. Diagnostic information is just one piece of the puzzle, and there is no substitute for relationships of trust in understanding all the youth you serve.

Parents as Partners

Knowledge and relationships go a long way in understanding youth with neurological differences, but living with them brings an even greater understanding. An essential ingredient in getting to know these young people is relying on their parents for guidance, support, and recommendations. Parents can warn you about triggers, inform you about what has happened in the past, and help you understand what classroom accommodations will be most helpful for their son or daughter. Take, for example, a student who has difficulty with self-regulation and is prone to meltdowns. Asking the parents (and the student!) what the typical causes of the meltdowns are, as well as their best strategies to prevent or respond to meltdowns, gives invaluable information for working with the student. Using a parents-as-partners model for your program will be invaluable as you build an inclusive community.

As you plan to include youth with special needs, consider the challenges their parents face. In many ways having a child with neurological differences can be extremely difficult. Feelings of disappointment, confusion, and frustration are common. As one parent shared about her experiences before her son came to Monarch: "You mourn, because you don't see your dream for your child as possible anymore. It is the death of your child: the death of the child you thought he was going to be."

Many aspects of these youths' lives are affected: friendships, marriages, finances, and often emotional health. The last thing they need is rejection from their faith communities.

When you welcome these families and commit yourself to understanding and serving their sons and daughters, you bring hope to those who may have lost hope. You provide an oasis, a respite from the stress of the struggle these families face daily. The previously quoted parent also shared, "Because of Monarch, we now see a future for our son. We no longer mourn for him." We at The Monarch School encourage you to invest in the future of these young people by welcoming them into your communities. In so doing, their presence will bless your communities.

5

Preparing the Soil: Hearts and Minds

Potatoes or petunias? Soil preparation varies dramatically, depending on what you plan to grow. Preparation of your catechetical environment (the hearts of the people, your gathering areas, and classrooms) will also be affected by the characteristics of the youth you serve. Although this chapter and chapters 6 and 7 include general tools and guidelines to help you build positive, supportive environments for all the young people in your programs, we encourage you to maintain an ongoing commitment to tailoring the environments to match the needs of specific young people in your community.

This commitment will be much easier with the support of the community. Good, clear communication of the beliefs, goals, and plans for the program will prevent misunderstandings and empower the congregation to support this work.

Spreading the Good News

One of the first steps is to share the vision with the entire community. This sharing can have added emphasis when it is done in conjunction with the regular Sunday worship.

Resource 5–A, "Sample Talk," is an example of a talk the pastor, director of religious education, or youth minister could give to the congregation. You are welcome to use this resource as a model, inserting details specific to your community. You could also send it as a letter to the congregation or include it in a weekly bulletin. Perhaps all three!

Signing Up

Getting to know the youth in your program begins with their registration. By adding a special needs questionnaire to the parent registration form, you will sometimes get a sneak preview of the youth who will be attending. This information can be invaluable in the choices you make for modifications.

Parents will not always choose to share the special needs of their sons or daughters. They may have had bad experiences with other organizations that were not as welcoming. They may not consider the catechetical or youth group experience as academic and so may not include issues such as learning disabilities or attention differences.

To encourage parents to share this information, it is helpful to include in the special needs section of the registration a statement of inclusion, such as the following:

This information is used to provide special accommodations and catechist awareness and does not influence admission decisions. We at [insert your community's name] are committed to including everyone and are eager to serve young people who have neurological, emotional, or physical differences.

There are several ways to solicit the special needs information. One way is to insert a general "special needs" statement, such as the following:

Please note any special needs your son or daughter may have, such as (but not limited to) learning or neurological differences, physical disabilities, allergies, existing illnesses, previous serious illnesses, injuries, or hospitalizations in the last twelve months, and any medication prescribed for long-term, continuous use.

The advantages to this approach include brevity, provision of a catchall question that can include virtually all possible special needs, and removal of the stigma sometimes associated with neurological differences by including them with physical and wellness issues. The disadvantage to this approach is the exclusion of young people who have special needs but have not received a diagnosis. Without the label parents are not as likely to share the characteristics.

An approach that can address undiagnosed issues would include questions in the areas representative of special needs symptoms, without the diagnostic labels, such as the following:

Does your daughter or son. . .
- have difficulty staying focused? Is she or he easily distracted?
- have serious problems with organization and responsibility?
- have difficulty in social interactions?
- have difficulty regulating her or his emotions?
- sometimes become emotionally overwhelmed or have meltdowns?

The weakness of this approach is the impossibility of considering and asking questions pertaining to all possible symptoms that may occur in the many different areas of special needs. Youth with trichotillomania might go unrecognized if only the questions above were asked. A thorough, combined approach with both general and specific questions is the most likely to yield complete results.

Although no shame should be associated with these special needs, it is important to respect the privacy of the families, so include in the registration that the information the parents share will remain confidential and will be shared only within your catechetical team. Then be deliberate about training the team to respect confidentialities.

Going Beyond the Labels

Identification of special needs involves a risk of creating an "us versus them" or "normal versus special" dichotomy in the community. Promoting the healthier and more realistic views of varied strengths and weaknesses in all of us will result in more support and understanding for your efforts and programs.

The following Beyond the Labels Workshop, for catechists and other leaders, can be used with various adult groups in your community. Resource 5–B "Celebrity Case Studies," and handout 5–A, "Diagnosis Information," can be used in the workshop. You could present the workshop to the pastoral council or board of education in an effort to increase support for your program, as well as to encourage special needs sensitivity throughout all parish programs. Presenting the session to catechists as part of their training will help them apply modifications to all the youth in their care rather than just those labeled with a special need. The workshop is also a powerful tool to present to youth as part of an introduction to your catechetical program, opening their eyes to see we all have some weaknesses in our abilities to learn, organize, and interact socially.

Beyond the Labels Workshop

Objectives
- to teach basic symptoms of seven neurological disorders
- to address the benefits, limits, and concerns regarding the use of diagnostic labels for special needs
- to emphasize that all of us have strengths and weaknesses that could be seen as special needs
- to reinforce the importance of accepting others as they are and not making assumptions about them based on labels

Activity A: Welcome and Introductions

Activity B: Celebrity Labels

Preparation
Materials
Gather the following items:

- ☐ five to ten PowerPoint photos or hard copies of celebrity photos that will elicit stereotypical responses such as "cool," "nerd," or "jock," as well as a TV or projection screen for displaying PowerPoint photos if used
- ☐ pens or pencils, one for each participant
- ☐ paper, one piece for each participant, numbered and with space for writing to correspond to the number of celebrity images shown

Process

1. Explain that you will show five to ten PowerPoint slides or hard-copy photos of well-known characters or celebrities from TV and movies. Choose a variety of individuals who will elicit a range of responses such as "nerd," "cool," "ditzy," and so forth. For example, a photo of Frank Sinatra could receive a variety of labels, ranging from "cool crooner" to "corny" or even "gangster."

2. Distribute a pen or pencil and a piece of numbered paper to each participant. Ask the participants not to put their names on their papers. As you show each photo, invite the participants to silently write labels on their papers. For those with difficulty writing by hand (dysgraphia), slow mental processing, or other issues that might make recording the labels difficult, you might want to pair them with a partner to whom they can whisper their labels to record.

3. After all the photos have been shown and the participants have finished recording their labels, collect the papers, mix them up, and then distribute them again at random. Show the photos again, one at a time, inviting the participants verbally to share the labels on the sheets with the large group.

4. As the participants read the labels for each celebrity, track and comment on the similarities, differences, trends, and so on. In some cases you likely will see recurrent themes. In other case, the labels will differ dramatically. Consider the variety of labels you might hear for controversial celebrities, such as pop stars like Britney Spears or political figures like the president of the United States. Stress how the same person may receive different labels, depending

on the viewer's background, preferences, or point of view. For example, when viewing a photo of Janis Joplin, some people might see a talented musician, whereas others may see a tragic drug addict. When these differences surface, steer the discussion in the direction of recognizing that labels are often subjective and the stuff of gossip and prejudice. Labels are limited in their ability to communicate truth about an individual.

Activity C: Who Wants to Go Shopping?

In preparation for this activity you will need sheets with sticky labels on them (narrow address labels work best). Print on the labels names someone might have been called when they were in school. Include labels such as the following: bookworm, bossy, brain, bully, class clown, cool, dreamer, goody two-shoes, gossip, head banger, holy roller, jerk, jock, know-it-all, loner, loud-mouth, mature, nerd, nice guy, nice gal, preppy, punk, rebel, responsible, shy, spoiled brat, teacher's pet, weirdo, wild, and wimp. You may want to enlist a few volunteer ahead of time to make the labels and brainstorm others that are not listed. Increase the fun by including humorous clip art with the wording on each label. Leave the labels on the larger sheets and scatter them around tables where participants can move around and reach them.

Preparation
Materials
Gather the following items:

- [ ] several sheets of sticky address labels
- [ ] several markers
- [ ] a six-sided die

Things to Do

- [ ] On the labels, print the names someone might be called in school, such as bookworm, bossy, bully, brain, nerd, and teacher's pet.
- [ ] You might enlist a few participants to make the labels, adding humorous clipart to them if you like.

Process

1. Tell the participants that all of us have received labels in our lives and that these labels can be positive or hurtful. Talk about a few labels you carried as a child—some that made you proud, as well as some that hurt. Be sure to share only information that is appropriate for the setting and the age-group

and only if you are comfortable sharing it. For example, you could share something like the following:

- o In second grade, I was labeled a nerd because each morning on the bus and at recess, I pointed out the specific types of clouds that happened to be in the sky that day: "And above that threatening cumulonimbus bank, you see the beautiful, featherlike cirrus clouds." I was very proud of this knowledge, but others saw my sharing as geeky. The label of nerd hurt me, although now I can see I earned it!

After sharing your labels, invite the participants to reflect on their childhoods and think about the labels they carried as young children.

2. Invite the participants to shop for labels. Explain that they will browse among the sheets of labels scattered on the tables. Their job is to choose ten labels others have used to describe them, then to peel off these labels and stick them on their shirts like name tags. For those who can't move around or who have difficulty moving around, you might want to print out a separate sheet with each of the labels on it.

3. After all the participants have finished shopping, invite them to take turns rolling a die and answering one of the following questions that corresponds to the number they roll. Keep in mind this may be personal for some people, so you may want to go over guidelines for appropriate sharing and responses from the group. These guidelines include sharing only what you are comfortable sharing and respecting others while they talk.

1. Which of these labels are you most proud to wear? Why?
2. Choose one of your labels and share one or two things you have done that have caused people to describe you that way.
3. Which of these labels is the most difficult for you to receive? Why?
4. Choose a label that represents a misunderstanding between how others see you and how you see yourself.
5. Describe each label in positive terms.
6. Answer any of questions 1–5.

Activity D: The Power of Labels

Facilitate a discussion of the power of labels, how they can have a positive or negative effect on a person's well-being and accomplishments, and how they ultimately fall short of describing the whole person. Lead with questions like the following:

- o How did these labels affect you when you were younger?
- o How did your childhood labels influence your growth and development?

- o Did your labels fully sum up who you were?
- o Do those childhood labels still affect your life as an adult?

Consider with the group how difficult these labels can be for a developing child. Relate the experience of children who are diagnosed with and receive labels such as autism, Tourette's syndrome, or bipolar disorder. Include how these diagnostic labels can be helpful in some ways (receiving appropriate treatment, connecting with others in support groups) but also can be limiting or even hurtful in others. Include a general discussion of stigma and how it affects a person's ability to function and to take ownership of his or her own goals and growth.

Activity E: Diagnoses of the Rich and Famous

Preparation
Materials
Gather the following items:

- ☐ a copy of resource 5–B, "Celebrity Case Studies," cut apart along score lines (When copying resource 5–B before the session, you may wish to hide the acknowledgments at the bottom of each case study to preserve the secret identity of each celebrity.)
- ☐ five copies of handout 5–A, "Diagnosis Information"
- ☐ PowerPoint photos of Abraham Lincoln, Dan Aykroyd, Howie Mandel, John Nash, and Jean-Claude Van Damme, as well as a TV or projection screen for displaying if used

Process
1. Divide the large group into five small groups and provide each small group with a copy of resource 5–B, "Celebrity Case Studies," along with a copy of handout 5–A, "Diagnosis Information."

2. Ask each group to read its case study and decide which diagnosis best fits their study. Allow 5 to 10 minutes for the groups to complete their diagnoses.

3. Bring the smalls groups together into the large group. Invite each small group to share its case study and diagnosis with the large group.

4. After each group shares its case study and diagnosis, reveal the celebrity identities. If you wish further dramatization, display PowerPoint photos of each

individual as he is revealed. The case study personalities and their diagnoses are as follows:

- o Abraham Lincoln, major depression
- o Dan Aykroyd, autism (Asperger's syndrome), Tourette's syndrome
- o Howie Mandel, obsessive compulsive disorder
- o John Nash, schizophrenia
- o Jean-Claude Van Damme, bipolar disorder

5. After the final group report, lead a reflective large-group discussion on the case study activity. Some possible discussion or reflection questions follow:

- o Were you surprised by the identity of the individual in your case study?
- o How does this activity affect your understanding of neurological differences?
- o How might a diagnostic label have affected the experiences of these individuals?

6. Close by stressing that we all have great potential to affect the world, regardless of our differences or limitations. Encourage the participants to see the person, not the diagnosis. Instead of seeing an autistic child, encourage them to see a child who happens to have autism. This difference in language may seem like a small matter, but it can make a powerful difference in how others see and interact with those who have these diagnoses. There is so much more to these young people than their diagnoses, and the way we refer to these youth affects how we and others perceive them.

Sample Talk

Good morning,

As you know our community is devoted to hospitality for all who enter through our doors. We are committed to a warm spirit of welcoming for everyone. It is especially important to extend this hospitality to our youth. When children approached Jesus, and the disciples tried to shoo them away, Jesus rebuked the disciples, and said, "No, let the children come."

We too say, "Let the children come." We want to be able to say that to all the youth of our community. Because of this strong desire, we are devoting ourselves to learning more about serving young people with special needs. We recognize that each youth is a unique creation of a loving God, with both strengths and weaknesses. We recognize that some youth have differences that may make participating in a community difficult for them.

Some of our young people may have learning differences, like dyslexia. We are committed to providing modifications to help them learn in ways that work for them.

Some of our young people may have attention differences, like attention deficit/hyperactivity disorder (ADHD). We are committed to structuring our lesson plans and learning spaces to help maintain focus, limit distractions, and decrease impulsivity.

Some of our young people may have autism, which affects their ability to interact socially. We are committed to providing support to help them grow in their relationship development.

If you are a young person with Tourette's syndrome, and you sometimes make unusual noises in the middle of class, you are welcome!

If you are a young person who has trouble controlling your emotions, and you sometimes get really angry, you are welcome!

If you are a young person with ADHD, and you can't sit still for five seconds, you are welcome!

If you are a young person . . . you are welcome. We accept you just the way you are. We are committed to providing a safe place for you to learn and grow.

Parents, when you register your sons and daughters for our program, you'll notice that the registration form includes some special needs questions. Our intention is not to be intrusive. This simply is the first step in our getting to know your children. When you share the information with us in this form, we'll follow up with a phone call to discuss in more detail the ways we can best serve your sons and daughters.

Do you have a background in special education, psychology, or another field that gives you expertise that could help us help our kids with special needs? We would love to have your support as we continue to learn and grow.

Do you love kids and want to volunteer in our program? We would love to have you help us.

I want to thank all of you for your attention and support as we work toward the goal of welcoming all God's children and continuing to say, "Let the children come." We'll be in the parish hall to answer any questions you may have about the program or if you would like to sign up to help. Thank you.

Celebrity Case Studies

Case Study 1

The following quotation comes from the man described in this case study:

> "I am now the most miserable man living. If what I feel were equally distributed to the whole human family, there would not be one cheerful face on the earth. Whether I shall ever be better I cannot tell; I awfully forebode I shall not. To remain as I am is impossible; I must die or be better, it appears to me."

This man was subject to frequent periods of sadness. He was said to frequently be in a gloomy mood, often wandering off into the woods with his gun, avoiding all contact with others. Friends reported that he frequently talked about thoughts of suicide and that the friends sometimes had to lock him up to keep him safe.

(The quotation by Abraham Lincoln on this resource is from the *Abraham Lincoln Research Site*, at *home.att.net/~rjnorton/Lincoln84.html*, accessed March 16, 2008.)

- - - - - - - - - - - - - - - - - - - -

Case Study 2

This man was born with webs between his toes, and his eyes are two different colors. Throughout his childhood, he made unusual noises or twitched in unusual ways.

In his school years, he had many problems getting along with other children, resulting in frequent outbursts in class. At one point he was expelled from school because of this.

He went on to study criminology at Carleton University, in Ottawa, Canada, but did not receive a degree. In 1994 he received an honorary doctor of literature degree from Carleton University.

From a very young age, this man has had an obsession with police work and now as an adult refuses to go anywhere without his replica "police badge."

(The information about Dan Aykroyd on this resource is from "Comedian—and Writer—Dan Aykroyd," on the *Fresh Air* radio program, National Public Radio, November 22, 2004.)

Case Study 3

At his work, this man meets new people every day, but he won't shake their hands. He prefers instead to bump knuckles.

His fear of germs is intense. He shaves his head because having a bald head makes him feel cleaner.

Because he travels about two hundred days a year, he often has to stay in hotel rooms. Before checking in, he requests twenty towels to cover the carpet for him to walk on. He also uses ice tongs to pull back the bedspread.

He purchased a second house, which he keeps sanitized, for him to retreat to whenever he feels overwhelmed living with his family in his primary home.

- -

Case Study 4

This man, a brilliant mathematician, was subject to paranoid delusions and spent 12 years of his life in and out of mental hospitals. He experienced both auditory and visual hallucinations. In response to his reactions to these experiences, the academic community sidelined him and his wife divorced him.

After his first hospital visit to treat his condition, his paranoia intensified, and he could no longer work. He went to Europe, wandering from city to city. He feared he was being spied on and hunted down, and he tried to give up his U.S. citizenship.

Looking back, he was able to see clues to his condition in his early behavior. He points to" . . . some decisions that might not have been the most rational, times I didn't follow the norm, thought differently. But I can see the connection between not following normal thinking and doing creative thinking. I wouldn't have had good scientific ideas if I had thought more normally."

Later in his life he was able to overcome his mental illness, learning to differentiate between what was real and what he imagined.

(The quotation by John Nash on this resource is from an interview at *www.schizophrenia.com/sznews/archives/001617.html*, accessed March 16, 2008.)

Case Study 5

When this Belgian-born man was in his teens and yet undiagnosed, he tried to compensate for his severe mood swings through physical training in karate, ballet, and other pursuits.

"When I didn't train for a couple of days," he said, "I felt so low and nothing could make me happy."

Throughout his career he struggled with drug abuse and was divorced four times. As his fourth wife filed for divorce, she cited drug and spousal abuse. At one point this man came close to committing suicide but was able to turn his life around when he was diagnosed and began taking medication for his disorder.

As a result, he felt a big difference. "Boom! In one week, I felt it kick in," he said. "All the commotion around me, all the water around me, moving left and right around me, became like a lake."

(The quotations by Jean-Claude Van Damme on this resource are from www.*bipolar.about.com/cs/celebs/a/jeanclaude.htm*, accessed March 16, 2008.)

Diagnosis Information

Attention Deficit/Hyperactivity Disorder (ADHD)

- difficulty sustaining attention
- easily distractible
- blurting out or interrupting
- difficulty waiting
- excessive physical movement

Asperger's Syndrome (a form of autism)

- impaired relationship development
- difficulty interacting socially and emotionally
- delayed or impaired communication skills
- repetitive behaviors
- restricted interests

Bipolar Disorder

- periods of intense highs and euphoria, followed by periods of severe depression

Major Depression

- depressed mood
- loss of pleasure
- weight change
- sleep disturbance
- fatigue

Obsessive-Compulsive Disorder (OCD)

- obsessions (persistent, often irrational, and seemingly uncontrollable thoughts)
- compulsions (actions performed to neutralize the obsessions)
- obsessions and compulsions disruptive to everyday functioning

Schizophrenia

- delusions
- hallucinations
- disorganized speech
- disorganized or catatonic behavior
- negativity

Tourette's Syndrome

- multiple motor tics and one or more vocals tics present simultaneously
- tics occur many times a day or intermittently over more than a year, without a tic-free period of more than a month
- age of onset less than 18 years
- symptoms not due to effects of a substance or general medical condition

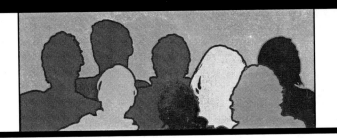

6

Preparing the Soil:
The Learning Environment

After having served our students on two rental properties for the last ten years, we at The Monarch School were delighted to break ground on our permanent school site in 2008. As we worked with the architects, we were able to design buildings and rooms to best meet the needs of all students, with consideration of room size, design, storage, lighting, acoustics, building materials, and numerous other concerns.

If your community has the opportunity to build, it will be helpful for you to research and consider these concerns as you plan. Most likely, though, you are working in a facility that may not have been designed for optimum learning. You can still make numerous modifications to transform the space into one that supports many different types of learners. Although many of your environmental modifications will come as a result of responding to the youth you serve, some general preparations are helpful for all learners.

Room Design

Traditional classrooms with rows of student desks facing the teacher's desk haven't worked well for many young people. Yet there is no one classroom design that is best for all learners. The key to good classroom layout is consideration of the many different tasks, groupings, and functions the learners may require.

As much as possible, the room should be designed for multiple purposes, with furniture that can be easily rearranged throughout the year to accommodate large-group and small-group interactions, learning areas that are separate from the larger areas, learning stations, and alternative seating.

Alternative Seating

The sisters who taught me in Catholic elementary and middle school required that every student stay in her or his desk, facing forward, with both feet on the floor. For some students this was not a problem. For other students, including me, this proved difficult, and we were frequently corrected for squirming, putting up our feet, or turning around in our seats. The goal of the strict standard was better learning, but the result was just the opposite. On some days the teacher spent more time controlling our posture than teaching the lessons, and many missed the lessons because of our anxiety or intense concentration on maintaining the appropriate posture.

Doesn't it make more sense to sit or stand in the way that best enhances learning, rather than staying seated with both feet on the floor and learning little? We all learn differently, and our sitting style is connected to our learning style. Some students learn best sitting in a chair in the traditional fashion. Other students learn better with their feet up. Some learn better sitting in a beanbag chair. Some learn better standing, some lying on the floor. As long as their sitting styles do not distract or disrupt others, why in the world would we not allow these variations? We should not only *allow* them but also *encourage* the youth to sit or stand in ways that work best for them.

Yes, this privilege can be abused and can be problematic. And yes, catechists must guide and regulate alternative seating to make it successful. Similarly catechists can coach students as they experiment with different postures and encourage alternatives if the current seating doesn't work.

Alternative seating is best introduced when students are calm and before there is a problem. If a student has lost focus, is upset, or is having a meltdown, introducing new seating alternatives in response is likely to be seen as critical or punitive and result in greater upset.

Additional seating alternatives you might consider include the following:

- study carrels—tables or desks with three dividers extending above the writing surface to serve as partitions, for youth with high levels of distractibility
- carpet squares—for individual seating on the floor; especially helpful for youth with autism, who can have difficulty with environmental boundaries
- rocking chairs—rocking movement can help some students focus or maintain calm
- hammock chairs—especially helpful for youth with a proprioceptive need for a feeling of high pressure around their bodies
- yoga balls—helpful for youth with vestibular issues

Lighting

Room lighting can make a significant difference in a young person's learning experience. As with other environmental factors, various lighting types and levels have different effects throughout the population. Bright lighting, especially direct sunlight or fluorescent lighting, can overwhelm some young people. Because dim lighting can also adversely affect some students' learning, teaching in a darkened classroom is not the answer.

As you design your classroom layout, use bookshelves, blinds, and shades to create a variety of differently lighted areas for young people to use, depending on their lighting preferences or needs. As much as possible, replace fluorescent lighting with incandescent free-standing lamps. Another helpful modification is to install dimmer switches.

Youth with visual-perception processing problems, such as Irlen syndrome, which is a perceptual disorder, have difficulty not only with bright lights but also with white surfaces. Research indicates that the use of color can significantly improve the learning experience for these young people.

Youth with visual-perception processing issues may benefit from the following modifications:

- Use Irlen colored overlays over reading material.
- Copy tests, handouts, and assignments on colored paper.
- Do written work on colored notebook paper.
- Place reading materials on an angle or use a book stand to reduce glare.
- Allow students to sit near a window or indirect lighting.
- Remove or turn off sections of lights.
- Let students wear hats with brims.
- Allow students to use fingers or markers to keep their places as they read.
- Use graph paper for math.
- Write in columns on the board.
- Use gray or brown erasable boards and avoid whiteboards.
- Use a colored overlay on an overhead projector.

These modifications may also help youth who do not have visual-perception processing problems, because colored filters have been shown to reduce eye strain, headaches, and migraines.

Classroom Organization

Virtually all learners benefit from a space that is organized and uncluttered. A messy, disorganized space can be a nightmare for some students. Organizing materials and supplies can be challenging, especially considering that many religious education classes are taught in shared, multipurpose spaces. To the highest degree possible, secure storage options for materials that are easily accessible but able to be closed off from view. Storage cabinets with shelving inside are preferable to open, visible shelves. Busy open shelves can, however, easily be hidden with a simple piece of fabric.

Rather than have materials scattered throughout the room, identify specific stations for different functions and storage. Each station should be identified visually with the title, as well as a symbol of the station's function. (Suggested symbols are listed in parentheses after the station names in the following paragraphs.)

At The Monarch School, our classroom organization relies heavily on the Treatment and Education of Autistic and related Communication-handicapped Children (TEACCH) program, centered in the Department of Psychology at the University of North Carolina at Chapel Hill. Even though the work of Gary Mesibov and his associates is geared primarily toward youth with autism, we have found the basic structure to be effective with virtually all young people.

Sensory Station (Station Symbol: Touching Hands)

Remember the story in chapter 1 about Carlos spinning the globe? For many young people with attention differences, a small squeeze ball can make a world of difference in their ability to focus. That same squeeze ball or stress ball could help youth with self-regulation issues, problems with anxiety, sensory integration difficulties, and many other challenges.

An essential feature in any learning space is a sensory station, which includes squeeze balls and other tools to help young people focus, calm themselves, organize thoughts, take breaks, and so on. The sensory station answers the executive function question, "What and where are the sensory tools the students need to function in this classroom?" An inexpensive, three-drawer plastic storage unit is perfect for the station. You can fill it with a variety of items, specific to the needs of your community or classroom.

Following is a list of suggested soothers, grouped by sensory needs. Within each sensory area, include a variety of sizes, colors, textures, and shapes. Use this as a jumping-off point and later individualize your sensory station based on the registration information, as well as the first few days of class with the youth.

Tactile Soothers

Include a variety of textures, because preferences and effectiveness will vary with each young person. A basic tactile soother drawer could include items such as the following:

- squeeze balls (for example, Koosh balls, both soft and firm, making sure they don't make a noise when squeezed)

- beanbags
- swatches of material (in texture from rough burlap to smooth silk or satin scarves)
- squares of carpet material
- sandpaper
- squares of hook-and-loop fasteners
- beads
- Flexi-sphere wire puzzles
- small pin-art squares
- Slinky spring toys
- Silly Putty or Theraputty modeling clay
- ribbon

Auditory Soothers

Auditory processing differences, as well as other neurological issues, are affected by loud or echoing environments but are accommodated through the use of tools such as the following:

- noise-reduction headphones (found inexpensively at sporting goods stores in the gun department)
- earplugs (individual, not shared; the foam type can also be purchased inexpensively at sporting goods stores)
- MP3 players with headphones, including a variety of music, white noise, nature sounds, and so on (CDs can be uploaded to MP3 players)
- mini tape recorders for the before-class or in-class recording of instructions or input

Visual Soothers

Variations in lighting style and intensity, room design, color patterns, and so forth affect visual processing differences and other neurological issues. The following tools may be helpful in accommodating visual challenges:

- sunglasses (include a variety of tints)
- translucent page overlays (include a variety of tints)
- cutout card stock "frames" (to limit amount of text visible at one time; can be taken from small photo frames purchased at dollar stores or cut from card stock)

Olfactory Soothers

Various aromas can influence issues such as self-regulation, mood, attention, and alertness and can include the following:

- blended essential oils on swatches of cloth (do not use pure oils, because they can be too strong)
- sprigs of plants such as lavender, peppermint, or rosemary

Olfactory soothers should be stored separately from other sensory items, because the aroma may transfer from one item to another. Use the soothers with great care and individualize them with parent permission; the scents may be overstimulating for some students, and some youth may be allergic to certain essential oils.

Proprioceptive and Vestibular Soothers

Proprioception is the sense of where the body and its parts are in relation to each other and the environment. *Vestibular* refers to equilibrium. For some young people, proprioceptive and vestibular differences can result in an appearance of clumsiness, running into things, falling down, knocking things over, and difficulty with fine-motor tasks. Soothers that can help with these challenges can include the following:

- weighted blankets
- weighted vests
- weighted neck wraps
- weighted lap pads

Oral Soothers

Chewing helps some youth stay calm and organized and is a good way to relieve stress. That's why you'll see many young people biting their fingernails or chewing on pens or pencils. With some young people (especially those with autism), this can extend to chewing sleeves, shirt collars, lips, tongues, papers, and textbooks. Chewing on a soother instead is a safer, more economical, and socially acceptable solution. You may want to include appropriate things to chew on in your sensory station like the following:

- chewing gum or hard candy
- chew tubes (the least expensive option is to buy either aquarium tubing or refrigerator tubing at a hardware store and cut it to appropriate lengths)
- drinking straws
- toothbrushes
- washcloths
- string

Obviously these items cannot be returned to the sensory station. Work out a plan for the hygienic storage and disposal of these items for identified personal use by only one child.

Use of Soothers

Ideally the youth in the classroom should have open access to the sensory station, taking ownership of their needs and modifications, retrieving, using appropriately, and returning soothers as needed. Teacher guidance and regulation of the station, however, are essential for this to work. Without a clear understanding of the uses and purposes of the soothers, young people may see them as toys to play with, as opposed to soothers to support them in their learning. Instead of a sensory station, you'll have a distracter depot!

Teach and demonstrate the appropriate use of soothers as part of the overall orientation to the course. Appropriate use should begin with a perceived problem (for example, distractibility, trouble reading, or difficulty understanding instructions). The youth should not go to the sensory station to shop for something. They should have a specific problem in mind for which they want to try to use a modification.

The first use of soothers for each young person should be viewed as an experiment, followed by reflection after the fact and a decision either to continue or discontinue the use.

Reflection Questions for Soother Use

Following a student's initial use of a soother, ask for and record answers to the following questions:

- What problem were you addressing?
- Did the soother improve the situation? If so, how?
- Did you use the soother appropriately?
- Was it a distraction to you or others?

Based on your answers and the answers of the young person, decide with the student whether to continue the use of the soother. If it was not effective, help the student choose another option. As the students become more responsible in using the sensory station, they can have more ownership of it. In the early stages, catechists should control access and require permission for the use of soothers.

Break Station (Station Symbol: Figure Sitting in Lotus Position)

In the adult world, breaks are common. We take coffee breaks, stretch our legs, or chat by the watercooler for a few minutes. Taking a brief period of time away from an extended task is helpful to us in reducing stress, maintaining focus, and staying alert. Sometimes these breaks are scheduled, but often they are spontaneous responses to stiffness, fatigue, distractions, and other causes.

The youth may experience these symptoms too, but often do not have the freedom to disconnect from a task for a few minutes to refuel, refocus, and refresh themselves. In most religious education classrooms, spontaneous, unscheduled breaks are not common. Some teachers believe young people are not responsible enough to have the freedom to take spontaneous breaks from classroom tasks. Our experiences at Monarch teaching youth with autism and other neurological differences have taught us that young people can be responsible enough to enjoy this privilege.

The break station answers the basic executive functioning question "Where and how do I take a break to refocus, refresh, or calm down?" Just like the sensory station, break plans can be individualized, depending on their effectiveness and appropriate use. Short, unscheduled breaks can benefit most students and are especially important for young people with attention, anxiety, and self-regulation issues. For those who have difficulty regulating their emotions, a break can keep upset from escalating to a full meltdown.

Because of supervision issues, it is not always possible for students to take breaks outside the classroom. Catechists can prepare a break area within the classroom for young people to use. This works best and is the least distracting if it is in the back of the classroom. If possible, use a room divider to create a visual barrier. The break area should be comfortable and can include beanbag chairs, blankets, pillows, and some soothers.

Because young people will use the break area for calming down when they are upset, it is crucial that the area not contain or be close to any objects or supplies that could cause physical harm, such as scissors, fold-up chairs, or free-standing lamps.

Use of the Break Station

Like the sensory station, the break area is not likely to be used appropriately without guidelines and regulation of its use. A clear explanation of its purpose and appropriate use should take place in the introductory session. Depending on the size of the break area and the characteristics of the young people in the class, the catechist should set clear rules regarding its use, including the total number of students allowed at one time, the granting of teacher permission (this should ultimately be individualized), and guidelines regarding interacting with other students while in the area.

The best use of this space begins when students recognize they are losing focus, feeling fatigued, or experiencing escalating anxiety or upset. In response to this recognition, they independently go to the break area for a few minutes and return to the class or gathering when they feel ready. There may be steps toward this ownership, though, beginning by requiring catechist permission and slowly moving toward spontaneous use as students demonstrate appropriate use of the break area.

Under no circumstances should the use of a break area be required of a student or used as a consequence for inappropriate behavior. The students' view of this tool would then shift to seeing it as a juvenile time-out, as opposed to an area to take a break from the class or gathering. If the catechist notices a need that a student doesn't, it is often helpful to suggest, but not insist on, a break to a student.

Stuff Station (Station Symbol: Backpack)

The stuff station answers the basic executive functioning question "Where do personal belongings go when students enter the classroom?" If students routinely bring personal belongings to your religious education classes, it will be helpful to have a specific station, preferably closable shelving or drawers, for students to store these belongings out of sight. This will reduce clutter and distraction during the lessons.

Information Station (Station Symbol: Lightbulb)

A special station in which all reference materials are stored will help your students know where to find information and be more autonomous in their work. The information station answers the basic executive functioning question "Where can students find the information they need to complete their work and better understand the lesson?" Bibles, biblical commentaries, Bible atlases, the *Catechism of the Catholic Church*, catechetical texts, and other resources could be included in the information station.

Supply Station (Station Symbol: Pencil)

Students searching and asking for needed supplies can be stressful to the classroom climate. Having a clearly marked and designated area for the storage of frequently used supplies, such as pencils, pens, glue sticks, highlighters, and so on, increases student ownership and reduces distractions in the classroom. This station answers the basic executive functioning question "Where are the classroom supplies stored?"

(Station titles and descriptions are from The Monarch School Operating Manual)

The Result of Organization

Organizing your religious education classroom to include these features will not only support youth with special needs in their learning but also will help all learners interact with one another and the environment, optimizing their success in the learning community. It's important to note that the assembly of these materials, structures, and systems can be challenging in time, effort, and expense. Making these changes over time is best, adding to and modifying them based on the needs of the youth who use the space.

7

Preparing the Soil: The Curriculum

Whether you're using a published curriculum or creating your own, considering individual differences and special needs will make your lessons more accessible to more youth. By integrating options into the lesson plans, you will be equipped with alternatives to provide for those youth who may not be developmentally capable of the activities and interactions described for the majority of the learners.

You can modify your lesson plans using the information from the registration form and from visiting with parents, as well as from the awareness and understanding you will acquire as you develop relationships with them.

As you review or create your lesson plans, consider and make allowances for developmental variances in the areas of learning, social interactions, self-regulation, and organization. Then integrate options into the lesson that accommodate these differences. Understand also that no matter how much time you spend planning accommodations within the lesson plans, there still will be surprises. The youth will struggle with aspects of the lessons that you may not have foreseen. Preparing lesson plans that are accommodating is the first step. It is equally important for catechists to be trained to respond to special needs as they become evident. This may seem daunting at first, but with practice, catechists will develop the tools to be able to spontaneously provide accommodations for all learners.

Criteria for Effective Lesson Plans

The typical collegiate model of "professor lecturing and students taking notes" is one of the least effective styles of teaching and learning. Even Socratic dialogue, containing a blend of lecture and discussion, favors the quick, verbal child and can exclude those who process or communicate more slowly.

Catechetical programs that follow the formula of "catechist reads the following to the class" without incorporating other methods are not only unproductive but also can be excruciatingly boring for the young people. The result of years of this type of instruction is often a mind-set that religion is boring. Only by providing fun, dynamic, and cooperative lessons can catechists transform religious instruction from "have to" into "want to."

As you review or compose lessons, it may be helpful to use the following set of questions as a rubric for enhancement of the curriculum.

Does the Lesson Plan Have an Experiential Component?

Meaning is derived by linking new information to previously learned knowledge or experience. For instance, when people taste a food they've never tried before and are asked to describe the flavor, they usually describe it by comparing it with other foods they've eaten.

In the same way, new information is best understood in a context the youth have already experienced. The key to developing an experiential component of a lesson plan is to identify a universal experience similar to the new input and to bring that experience to mind through reflection or activity. Ask yourself, What have most or all of the young people experienced that is similar to the information I'm about to present?

This is especially important when teaching abstract concepts. For example, look at the Sermon on the Mount and Jesus' use of salt as a metaphor for Christian presence in the world. Teaching middle school teens that they are the salt of the earth is not likely to yield much understanding. Ask yourself, What have all the youth experienced that will help them understand the metaphor of salt? From there it's a few easy steps to developing a powerful introductory experiential activity, such as the one that follows:

Experiential Activity

At the beginning of class, excitedly share that you have a special treat for everyone. Distribute small bags of unsalted popcorn. Give the students time to eat some of the popcorn; watch for reactions. Respond to any negative reactions with questions such as "What's wrong? Aren't you enjoying the popcorn? Doesn't it taste good?" Respond to any complaints by either salting the popcorn or giving the students new bags of salted popcorn. Then ask: "Is that better? Why do you like it better with salt? How does the salt make the popcorn better?" Now you have a bridge to concrete experience that will help the students understand that aspect of the metaphor.

A caution: the challenge of the experiential piece is to connect it to something that is nearly universally experienced, that is similar to the new information. It is not simply surveying the class for those who have already experienced the new information. Take an introductory dance course, for example.

The instructor might begin the class by asking: "How many of you have danced before? What was it like?" In this case the experience is not general enough to be shared by all. The experiential connection is limited to those who have already danced. Those who have never danced don't have an experiential connection. What would be a better, more universal experience that most, if not all, of the class has experienced? Perhaps sports or other activities that use similar gross motor skills or movements or tapping one's foot in time to music. The important thing is to identify something general enough to build on, to attach to the new information.

Is the Lesson Plan Participatory?

What was the most common teaching style in school when you were growing up? During that time what was your favorite teaching style? Most people who answer the first question say a teacher-centered, lecturing style was most common. Yet the same people usually do not choose this style as an answer to the second question. Many people enjoy a student-centered, hands-on teaching style. But lecture is common because it is easy. It is controlled. It is efficient. Note that lecture does have a place in good teaching, and some people prefer, and learn best with, a lecture style. But a style that is exclusively lecture can leave many students behind.

Young people learn best if they actively participate in their own learning. If your lesson plans currently contain too much teacher talk, find creative ways to modify the delivery of the content to be more participatory and interactive. Instead of telling the students the information, let them discover the same knowledge through the use of the following prompts:

- Turn to a neighbor and share . . .
- Raise your hand if you've ever . . .
- Who can share an example of . . .
- What do you notice in this . . .
- What do you already know about . . .
- Ask the person to your right the following . . .
- As you read or listen, look for . . .
- Applaud if you agree with . . .

In a participatory approach, the catechist functions as less of an information provider and more of a learning facilitator. This person always looks for ways to transfer the action of the learning to the students. Rather than being the sage on the stage, the catechist takes the role of guide on the side. The result is more and better learning and more student ownership.

Is the Lesson Plan Entertaining?

> Anyone who tries to distinguish between education and entertainment doesn't know the first thing about either. (Marshall McLuhan, from the BrainyQuote Web site)

This quotation from communications theorist Marshall McLuhan reminds us of the close relationship between education and entertainment. Consider the concern many parents and educators have about what young people learn from movies, video games, and so on. Even if it has no specific intent to educate, all entertainment has an educational aspect.

When some people suggest that education should be entertaining, others suggest that students are here to learn, not be entertained. Some educators resent having to compete with high-stimulation video games, movies, and other forms of entertainment. This is an appropriate and reasonable response if the youth are to be entertained as passive and sedentary recipients. It is less reasonable if the youth enthusiastically participate in an entertaining activity.

Ultimately, don't we want our lesson plans to be engaging and captivating? Efforts to make lesson plans more fun, amusing, and entertaining can make a significant difference in the learning experience. When young people are engaged in something they enjoy, their learning differences can have less effect. Parents of young people with attention differences that result in short attention spans are chagrined at the hours their children can remain glued to a screen of any kind. Simply put, we all learn better when engaged in something we enjoy.

Your tool chest for entertaining lesson plan designs and modifications can include the use of humor, multimedia presentations, role-playing, art, and games. Look at your lesson plans and ask yourself, How can I tweak this to make it more interesting, engaging, and entertaining?

Does the Lesson Plan Appeal to Different Senses and Learning Styles?

Beginning in the 1970s, educators began to recognize that learners varied in the ways they learned best. Many different theories outline various modalities of learning. Most people agree that people learn in the following ways:
- auditory (hearing)
- visual (seeing)
- kinesthetic (doing)

In other words, some youth learn best by listening, some by watching, and some by doing. Lesson plans that provide an overlap of learning styles will reach the most learners (for example, instructions both given orally and written on the board). Lessons can be enhanced by making them more hands-on, giving the youth the opportunity to learn by doing.

In most lessons sight and sound are the predominant senses the students use. You can enhance your lessons by also including the other senses: taste (as in the popcorn example), touch (with hands-on activities), and even smell!

In 1983 Dr. Howard Gardner, professor of education at Harvard University, developed the theory of multiple intelligences. Gardner's work is based on the belief that areas of intelligence measured by IQ tests (logical-mathematical and linguistic) are only a small part of our intelligence. Gardner has identified the following nine intelligences:

- linguistic intelligence (as in a poet)
- logical-mathematical intelligence (as in a scientist)
- musical intelligence (as in a composer)
- spatial intelligence (as in a sculptor or airplane pilot)
- bodily-kinesthetic intelligence (as in an athlete or dancer)
- interpersonal intelligence (as in a salesperson or teacher)
- intrapersonal intelligence (as in individuals with accurate views of themselves)
- naturalist intelligence (as in a botanist or biologist)
- existentialist intelligence (as in a philosopher or spiritual leader)

(*Intelligence Reframed*, pages 41–43 and 47)

Lesson plans commonly overemphasize linguistic intelligence. To reach more students, modify the activities to include a sampling of the other areas of intelligence. Using Gardner's intelligences as a guide, ask yourself questions like, How could I incorporate music into this lesson? Is there a way to give those with high spatial intelligence a way to learn this information through artwork? How can I incorporate physical movement into the lesson for those with high bodily-kinesthetic intelligence?

As Eugene Webb, cofounder of The Monarch School and author of the foreword of this book, says, "The more 'parts' of a child that are engaged, the richer the learning and the more enduring the memory."

Is the Lesson Plan Constructivist?

Constructivist simply means "Who is responsible for generating and communicating the knowledge attained in the lesson?" Traditional approaches locate the information or knowledge with the instructor, who imparts the knowledge to the students, with the information going from known (the teacher) to unknown (the students). This approach is reflected by images of teachers pouring knowledge into the brains of the students. A constructivist approach includes the teacher imparting knowledge to the student but also incorporates student-generated knowledge. Students and teachers build the knowledge together.

This approach recognizes that catechists can also learn from students and that students can learn from one another.

Does the Lesson Plan Apply to Real Life?

No matter how entertaining or captivating your lesson plan, if it isn't relevant in the lives of the students, it ultimately will have no lasting effect. When reviewing or creating lessons, ask yourself, How can students apply these concepts in their lives? Include out-of-class follow-up assignments that allow the students to practice the principles communicated in the lessons. For example, a lesson on forgiveness could include a challenge for reflection and action outside class: asking for or extending forgiveness, repairing broken relationships, or making restitution for harm done to individuals or the community.

Is the Lesson Plan Flexible?

A one-size-fits-all approach, which doesn't offer choices, will ultimately result in an ill fit for some students. Including options and choices in the lesson plans allows students more freedom in and ownership of their learning experiences. Choices enhance all the criteria for effective lesson plans, giving students the opportunity to choose methods that work best for them. Additionally, compulsory participation is likely to create anxiety in some students if their learning differences make a particular element of a lesson difficult for them.

For example, many lesson plans incorporate a reading circle, in which each student takes a turn reading aloud. For young people with difficulty reading aloud, this can be frightening and humiliating. As alternatives, modify the reading circle by making the reading optional, pairing students with a reading buddy, or allowing silent individual reading.

Similarly, when silent reading is called for, some youth need absolute quiet to read, so allow the use of noise-reducing headphones or reading in a private area. You can also provide co-readers so youth with reading difficulties won't just sit in silence, pretending to have read the material.

Flexibility during group activities is crucial, because social coordination is often the most challenging struggle for young people. In forming groups, consider the students' different levels of abilities and include options for individual projects or for groups of two or three students. Automatic group divisions, such as boys against girls, can present difficulties for students with social coordination challenges. Similarly, allowing the students to choose their own groups can result in some young people's being excluded.

Some lesson plans include written responses in a workbook. Students with dysgraphia or other difficulties that make this task challenging will benefit from options such as keyboarding their answers into a computer, pairing up with a buddy who can record the answers, or using a different medium altogether, such as drawing, to communicate the information.

Following are some examples for varying the options within a lesson:

- "For the next activity, you may work individually or form groups of two or more, up to four in each group."
- "For your group skit, you may be a performer, or if you prefer, you may take a behind-the-scenes role, such as the director."
- "As you listen to the music, you may read the lyric sheet, watch the images projected onto the screen, or just close your eyes and enjoy."

When designing a lesson, ask yourself, Without severely interrupting the flow of the lesson, what alternatives can I offer to give the students choices based on their individual learning needs and preferences? The ultimate flexibility will provide for options that the students can choose during actual lessons.

Is the Lesson Plan Innovative?

Creativity is crucial for developing engaging lesson plans. If students have been there, done that, they aren't likely to be captivated. Rather than include another trust walk, for example, dream up novel activities. Reject the first thing that comes to mind in favor of the second or third, more creative, idea. For example, when designing a prayer service to be included in a lesson plan on gratitude, the first idea might be "Let's all stand in a circle and share one thing we are thankful for." Let that one go and keep thinking. Exercise those creative muscles! The second idea might be "Let's think about our many blessings and write a thank-you note to God." Getting warmer! What would your third, more creative idea be? Dig deep and develop lessons that provide the youth with unique experiences they can really sink their teeth into. You can also take a time-honored, classic activity and tweak it with a unique variation. As you develop lesson plans, ask yourself: How can I modify these to be more unique? What quirky additions can I include to increase their novelty?

Options, Openness, and Opportunity

A rigid curriculum that requires all the youth to do the same thing in the same way may appeal to you for its ease and simplicity. The complexity of a multi-option, open system with lots of opportunities for individualized instruction may seem daunting and difficult. But Dr. Neal Sarahan tells us: "We advocate for all students to be engaged, all to be served, all to be enjoying the adventure of discovering and living their faith. This is the unique gift of students with disabilities—they cause us to focus on learning and teach us how to reach them."

8

Gathering and Training the Workers

Use this chapter in combination with chapter 7 to facilitate catechist training in criteria for excellence in religious education. It covers the first four lesson criteria from chapter 7, as follows: experiential, participatory, entertaining, and flexible. Each component of the training in chapter 8 is designed to give the catechists a good understanding of the meaning and application of the different criteria. The training is designed as a full day but can be broken up into modules, with the different sessions being presented separately.

For each session you will find a list of needed supplies. The sessions included are as follows:

- QuickStart Activities (as participants arrive)
- Session One: Experiential
- Session Two: Participatory
- Session Three: Entertaining
- Session Four: Flexible
- Session Five: Reflection

QuickStart Activities
Q and A

Preparation
Materials
Gather the following items:

☐ index cards, one for each participant, each with one of the following questions on it:

- How can I feel less nervous when ministering to youth?

- What should I do when I ask a sharing question, and nobody volunteers?

- How should I respond when a student asks me a question I can't answer?

- Should I change plans on the spur of the moment if I don't think something is working, or is it better to stick to the script?
- How do I handle students who talk too much? not enough?
- How much should I speak during the lesson, and how much should the youth speak?
- How long should I spend preparing for each class?

☐ pens or pencils, one for each participant

☐ flip chart with the question "What do you want from this catechist training?" written on one page and the question "What can you contribute to this catechist training?" written on another page

☐ markers for writing on flip charts

Process

1. As the catechist participants enter, distribute an index card and a pen or pencil to each. Ask the participants to mingle and ask their questions of one another, gathering the wisdom of the group and jotting down notes on the backs of their cards.

2. When the participants are done mingling, read aloud the first question from the flip chart:

○ What do you want from this catechist training?

Have the participants write their answers on the chart. Then read the second from the flip chart:

○ What can you contribute to this catechist training?

Likewise, ask the participants to write their answers on the chart.

3. Pause the activity and welcome the participants to the session. Let them know the schedule for the day and a general overview of what they can expect. Also include information about tending to basic needs like bathroom locations, food, breaks, and so on. Give permission for the participants to participate fully or simply to withdraw and observe.

4. Read aloud (or invite the participants to share) some of the answers on the flip chart pages. You may also ask the participants to share some of the notes they wrote on their question cards while mingling with the other participants at the beginning of the activity.

Sharing Our Experiences

Process

1. Pair the participants. Ask the pairs to discuss this question:
   o What is the best experience you have had when speaking in front of a group?

2. When pairs are done discussing, invite large-group retelling of these experiences:
   o Who heard a terrific story they'd like to invite their partner to share with the larger group? You may hear possible additions to the "What can you contribute?" question on the flip chart. If so, respond with something like:
   o Sounds like you're really good at _____. May I add that to our list of ways you will contribute?

3. Form the participants into groups of four. Ask them the following question:
   o What is the worst experience you have had when speaking in front of a group?

4. After the small groups have finished discussing, invite large-group retelling of these experiences:
   o Would you like to invite someone in your group to share his or her story with all of us?

   You may hear possible additions to the "What do you want?" question on the flip chart. If so, respond with something like:
   o Sounds like you experience some nervousness when teaching. Have you written that down on the flip chart as something you want to focus on in this workshop?

5. Affirm the group for sharing stories. Mention a few that were particularly significant. Also express that one of the day's purposes is to increase the positive experiences of catechists through focusing on skills and criteria that contribute to outstanding catechesis.

Session One: Experiential

Preparation

Materials
Gather the following items:

☐ a plastic bag filled with jelly-smeared grapes
☐ an unusual drink, such as guava juice, poured into three or four small cups

☐ an interesting photo or portrait of a person
☐ premoistened hand towels (for use after touching grapes and jelly)

Process

1. Have the participants reach into the bag prepared with the jelly-smeared grapes one at a time. Ask them what it feels like. Request a different answer from each person. Provide premoistened hand towels for participants to clean their hands after touching the grapes.

2. Provide an unusual drink for three or four participants to taste. Ask them what it tastes like. Request different answers from each person.

3. Have the participants look at the photo or portrait. Ask them whom it looks like. Request a different answer from each person.

4. Identify and define *experiential* as the first criterion for an exceptional catechetical presentation. (See chapter 7.) Ask the participants why they think it's first. Explain that it is the beginning point for all learning.

Discuss how new ideas must be linked to previously learned ideas to be understood fully. Explain that the participants figured out what they were experiencing with the grapes, drinks, and portrait by relating feeling, taste, and visual to other things the participants had experienced in the past.

Discuss the use of similes and metaphors to create understanding in literature. Sometimes authors explain new things by relating them to familiar things, such as, "Her hair was like flaxen wheat, blowing in the breeze." Brainstorm slogans and songs that reflect this principle, such as the song "Like a Rock" being used to sell trucks or "Like a Rolling Stone" being used to describe someone who doesn't stay in one place for long.

5. Divide the large group into small groups of four. Invite each small group to choose a topic for a catechetical lesson. Provide examples like the one below. After each group has chosen a topic, have the members brainstorm a list of experiences connected to the topic. Invite each small group to design and present a brief introductory experiential activity to the large group.

Example Topic and Experiential Activity

Topic: Scriptural Story of Jesus' Walking on the Water
Following is a list of experiences like Peter's when Jesus invited him to walk on the water:

- riding a bike for the first time
- speaking in front of a large audience

- trying to get the nerve to dive from a high dive
- feeling nervous before an important exam
- starting a new job

Turn to a neighbor and share a story of a time when someone encouraged you to try something that involved risk. How did you feel? How did the other person help you make the attempt? What happened? Did you succeed or fail?

Be sure the participants understand that the experiential part of the lesson cannot be the same experience as the new information. In a classroom lesson, the goal is to tap into something that virtually all the youth have experienced and then to use that experience to attach the new information. You wouldn't begin the example lesson by asking, "By a show of hands, how many of you have walked on water?" Further illustrate the point with the example of a lesson on salt of the earth. You wouldn't ask, "How many of you have worked in a salt mine?" Choose something more universally experienced, like eating salted foods. Explain that the experiential part of the lesson has to be something like the new input, not simply different experiences of the new input.

Session Two: Participatory

Preparation

Materials
Gather the following items:

☐ a chalkboard or white board
☐ a piece of chalk or a dry-erase marker
☐ resource 8–A, "Fun Facts About Saints," cut apart into individual slips
☐ a hat or other receptacle to hold the slips with fun facts

Process

1. Tell the group you will present a lesson on autism. Then read the following in a slow, monotonous tone:

   o Autism is a complex developmental disability that typically appears during the first three years of life and is the result of a neurological disorder that affects the normal functioning of the brain, impacting development in the areas of social interaction and communication skills. Both children and adults with autism typically show difficulties in verbal and nonverbal communication, social interactions, and leisure or play activities. One should keep in mind, however, that autism is a spectrum disorder, and it affects each individual differently and at varying degrees—this is why early diagnosis is so crucial. When adults learn the signs, a child can begin benefiting from one of the many specialized intervention programs. Autism is one of five disorders that falls under the umbrella of pervasive developmental disorders (PDD), a category of neurological disorders characterized by "severe and pervasive impairment in several areas of development" (Autism Society of America Web site).

2. Finish the reading, then look up and, with a flat facial expression, silently scan the faces in the room. Ask the group how the lesson made them feel. After several answers, tell the group you're going to try a different approach.

3. Invite a volunteer to act as a recorder at the board and then conduct a brisk, information-gathering walk among the participants, asking for volunteers to share one fact they know about autism. After each contribution smile and say something like, "Good, let's add that to our list!" or "Excellent contribution; let's capture that knowledge on the board!"

4. After the brainstorming session, stop and once again scan the faces in the room. Ask the group how that experience made themfeel.

5. Ask:
o Which style—lecture or interactive—did you like better? Why?
o What was the most common teaching style you experienced in school? (The likely response will be lecture.)
o What was your favorite teaching style? (The likely response will be hands-on or interactive.)

6. Invite the participants to turn to a neighbor and explore why lecture is the most common delivery style even though it is typically the least favorite learning style. (Potential answers: It's easy. It's safe. It's controlled. It's efficient.) Invite the participants to share interesting answers they hear from their partners.

7. Ask when a hands-on style of delivery is most appropriate, when a lecture style is most appropriate, and when a combination of the two is best.

B. Fun Facts About Saints

Invite the participants to come to the board and each draw a fun facts slip from the hat. Ask the participants to develop ways to teach the fact's content in a creative, participatory way to the larger group. Allow the participants to develop their ideas with partners if they wish.

Session Three: Entertaining

Preparation

Materials
Gather the following items:

☐ copies of handout 8–A, "Teaching an Entertaining Lesson," one for each small group of four or five
☐ handout 8–B, "Criteria for Excellent Lessons"
☐ a chalkboard or white board
☐ a piece of chalk or a dry-erase marker

A. Education and Entertainment

1. Write the first half of this Marshall McLuhan quotation on the board: "Anyone who tries to distinguish between education and entertainment . . ."

2. Ask volunteers how they would finish the statement.

3. After several participants share, complete the quotation on the board: ". . . doesn't know the first thing about either" (found at the BrainyQuote Web site).

4. Ask the following questions:

   o Do you agree with McLuhan's statement? Why or why not? What do you think McLuhan meant by this?

   o Do you like this quotation? Some people don't like it. Why do you think that is?

5. Discuss the traditional value of "You're here to learn, not be entertained." Discuss the frustration teachers feel when they are expected to entertain students in competition with high-stimulation video games, movies, and so on.

6. Share the following definition with the participants:

   o **en • ter • tain**

      1. to hold the attention with something amusing or diverting
      2. to extend hospitality toward: *entertain friends at dinner*
      3a. to consider; contemplate: *entertain an idea*
      3b. to hold in mind; harbor: *entertained few illusions*

   [*The American Heritage Dictionary of the English Language*, fourth edition]

7. Conduct a general discussion with the participants, using the following questions:

- o How does the climate and hospitality of a classroom affect learning?

- o What is the potential long-term effect of uncreative, tedious religious instruction?

- o What are the worst and best religious education experiences you have ever had?

8. Tell the participants we usually remember the best and the worst, but we don't remember the majority of experiences that were nondescript, bland, and, therefore, totally forgettable! Try to encourage balance in recognizing that although catechists don't have to produce a Broadway play each class period, they should try to present lessons that are captivating and entertaining. Make the point that the students in class must be involved in the entertaining aspects, rather than passively watching entertaining features.

9. At an appropriate point in the discussion, pose the following question:
- o Are there some subjects you cannot teach in an entertaining way? Why or why not?

10. Share with the group that, no matter the topic, teaching it in an entertaining way is possible.

11. Divide the large group into small groups of four or five to plan and present brief lessons for teaching difficult content in an entertaining way.

12. Distribute the copies of handout 8–A. Invite the small groups to choose one of the three lesson topics. Give the groups 20 minutes of preparation and practice time.

13. Invite each small group to entertain the larger group with its lesson.

14. After each presentation invite the "audience" to join in identifying creative ways the small groups made their lessons entertaining.

Session Four: Flexible

Process

1. Using the same small groups and lesson topics from the previous activity, challenge the small groups to identify modifications and accommodations for the various developmental differences of the young people they are teaching. Each group is responsible for brainstorming several ways to accommodate or modify the lesson plans for their topic to include each of the following special needs:

- difficulty staying focused
- difficulty coordinating in groups larger than two
- high sensitivity to loud noises
- high sensitivity to light
- slow processing skills
- difficulty reading
- problems calming down when excited
- difficulty with sequential instructions (can process and respond to only one step at a time)
- difficulty receiving visual or auditory input
- short attention span

2. When the groups finish brainstorming, gather everyone into the large group and celebrate the participants' openness to flexibility in the classroom. Discuss the logistical, emotional, and social challenges involved in a flexible curriculum. Refer back to the easier, more efficient method of requiring all participants to learn in only one way and the inevitable exclusion that occurs with this approach. Encourage the participants to choose the more difficult path of including everyone!

Session Five: Reflection

Process

1. Invite the participants to spread out around the room and spend some quiet time in reflection.

2. After about 5 minutes, begin a reflection discussion, asking the following questions and inviting the participants to share their thoughts:
   o Has today's training changed how you view your role as a catechist? If so, how?
   o What principles, concepts, or techniques presented today stand out as particularly helpful to you in your role as catechist?
   o Did you strongly disagree with or have trouble accepting anything taught today? Please share your perspectives.
   o Will your teaching be different as a result of today's training? If so, how?
   o What are you curious to learn more about as a result of today's training?

Conclusion

As you conclude the training, distribute a copy of handout 8–B, "Criteria for Excellent Lessons" to each participant. Encourage the catechists to keep the list handy whenever preparing to teach a lesson and to continue to develop their teaching skills to provide for more exciting, engaging lessons for the youth. Stress that this improvement is a long journey rather than a quick fix and that they should focus on a few criteria at a time, slowly adding to their tool chest of teaching skills. Congratulate the participants and celebrate their commitment to spreading the Good News to our young people!

Fun Facts About Saints

Divine Detour

Saint Genevieve once stopped Attila the Hun from invading Paris by persuading the people to repent, fast, and pray rather than flee the city. When the praying started, Attila suddenly changed course, and the city was saved!

(This information is adapted from "Saints Fun Facts," at the Catholic Online Web site, at *www.catholic.org/saints/fun_facts_arch.php*, accessed March 16, 2008. Copyright © by Catholic Online, *www.catholic.org*. Used with permission of Catholic Online.)

Speaking with the Fishes

Saint Anthony of Padua was once so fed up with the hard-heartedness and heresies of the citizens of Rimini, Italy, he went to the town's riverbanks and preached to the fish instead! The townspeople thought they'd better listen too when they saw the multitudes of fish show up!

(This information is adapted from "Saints Fun Facts," at the Catholic Online Web site, at *www.catholic.org/saints/fun_facts_arch.php*, accessed March 16, 2008. Copyright © by Catholic Online, *www.catholic.org*. Used with permission of Catholic Online.)

Vincent the Innocent

Saint Vincent de Paul was once accused by his roommate, a judge, of stealing more than 400 crowns. (Crowns were a unit of money.) The saint replied that he was innocent, that he had been bedridden all day with illness, and that God knew the truth. Incensed, the judge spread his lie all over Paris. Sometime later, the real thief confessed. He had made a delivery to their residence, seen the money in the cupboard, and taken it. The judge was so embarrassed and frazzled by his mistake and his rumormongering that he instantly wrote a letter of apology to the great saint, offering to get down on his knees and beg forgiveness!

(This information is adapted from "Saints Fun Facts," at the Catholic Online Web site, at *www.catholic.org/saints/fun_facts_arch.php*, accessed March 16, 2008. Copyright © by Catholic Online, *www.catholic.org*. Used with permission of Catholic Online.)

Eat Your Heart Out, Nostradamus!

In the fifth century, Saint Nilus the Elder, a monk who lived on Mount Sinai, in modern-day Egypt, accurately foresaw the existence of aircraft, submarines, and telephones!

(This information is adapted from "Saints Fun Facts," at the Catholic Online Web site, at *www.catholic.org/saints/fun_facts_arch.php*, accessed March 16, 2008. Copyright © by Catholic Online, *www.catholic.org*. Used with permission of Catholic Online.)

Teaching an Entertaining Lesson

Bunions

If the joint that connects your big toe to your foot has a swollen, sore bump, you may have a bunion, a common deformity often blamed on wearing tight, narrow shoes, and high heels. More than half the women in America have bunions. Bunions may occur in families, but many come from wearing tight shoes. Nine out of ten bunions happen to women. Nine out of ten women wear shoes that are too small. Too-tight shoes can also cause other disabling foot problems like corns, calluses, and hammertoes.

With a bunion, the base of the big toe (metatarsophalangeal joint) enlarges and sticks out. The skin over it may be red and tender. Wearing any type of shoe may be painful. This joint flexes with every step. The bigger the bunion gets, the more walking hurts. Bursitis may set in. The big toe may angle toward the second toe, or even move all the way under it. The skin on the bottom of the foot may become thicker and painful. Pressure from the big toe may force the second toe out of alignment, sometimes overlapping the third toe. An advanced bunion may make the foot look grotesque. If the bunion gets too severe, walking may be difficult. The pain may become chronic and arthritis may develop.

Relief from bunions. Most bunions are treatable without surgery. Prevention, however, is always best. To minimize the chances of developing a bunion, never force the foot into a shoe that doesn't fit. Choose shoes that conform to the shape of the feet. Choose shoes with wide insteps, broad toes, and soft soles. Avoid shoes that are short, tight, or sharply pointed and those with heels higher than 2¼ inches. If a bunion is already present, wear shoes that are roomy enough not to put pressure on it. This should relieve most of the pain. Having the shoes stretched professionally may be a good idea. Protective pads may also cushion the painful area.

If the bunion has progressed to the point where walking is difficult or pain occurs despite accommodative shoes, surgery may be required. Bunion surgery realigns bone, ligaments, tendons, and nerves so the big toe can be brought back to its correct position. Orthopedic surgeons use several techniques to ease pain. Many bunion surgeries are done on a same-day basis (no hospital stay) using an ankle-block anesthesia. A long recovery is common and may include persistent swelling and stiffness.

Adolescent bunions. A young teenager (especially a girl ages ten to fifteen) may develop an adolescent bunion at the base of the big toe. Unlike adults with bunions, a young person can normally move the affected joint. The teenager may have pain and trouble wearing shoes. Try having his or her shoes stretched, or try buying wider shoes. Surgery to remove an adolescent bunion is not recommended unless the child is in extreme pain and the problem does not become better with changes in footwear. If the adolescent has bunion surgery, particularly before reaching full physical growth, there is a strong chance the problem will return.

Bunionettes. If a painful, swollen lump appears on the outside of the foot near the base of the little toe, it may be a bunionette (or a tailor's bunion). A hard corn and painful bursitis also may appear in the same spot. A bunionette is much like a bunion. Wearing shoes that are too tight may cause it. Get shoes that fit comfortably with a soft upper and a roomy toe box. In cases of persistent pain or severe deformity, surgical correction is possible.

(The information about bunions on this handout is adapted from "Bunions," at the American Academy of Orthopaedic Surgeons Web site, at *orthoinfo.aaos.org/topic.cfm?topic=A00155,* accessed March 16, 2008. Reproduced with permission from C.F. Moseley, editor, *Your Orthopaedic Surgeons.* Available at *orthoinfo.aaos.org*.)

Types of Hinges

A large variety of hinges is available from most hardware stores. The type needed depends on how the hinge is to be used and what it is to be fitted to. For example, when selecting a hinge for a jewelry box, a small brass butt hinge is likely to be used rather than a concealed hinge. Furthermore, brass hinges are more expensive than steel ones, because they give a quality look to the completed product. Following are some of the more popular hinges available:

Butt hinge. This type of hinge is most widely used for mounting ordinary doors. Butt hinges are available in both the rigid and loose pin type. The pin cannot be removed from the rigid butt hinge. The pin can be easily tapped out of the loose pin type with an ordinary screwdriver.

Butterfly hinge. This type of hinge is often used on lightweight doors. Different shapes and patterns are available. Butterfly hinges are generally easy to fit.

Flush hinge. This type of hinge does not require a recess to be cut. The flush hinge is primarily a cabinet hinge. It should be used only on light doors. You will probably prefer this type of hinge when you want to completely conceal every part of the hinge except the barrel.

Barrel hinge. This type of hinge comes in two parts. The threaded part of the hinge is screwed into a predrilled hole. Barrel hinges are easy to fit and can be dismantled.

Spring-loaded hinge. This type of hinge has a built-in spring mechanism that closes the door after each opening. Some models of spring-loaded hinges have adjustaable tension features that permit tightening or loosening the hinge, as for an ordinary door closer.

Continuous, or piano, hinge. This type of hinge comes in different lengths and in brass or steel. Continuous hinges are ideal where long hinges are required, such as a desktop or a cupboard door. Small countersink screws are normally used to fix them in position.

(The information about hinges on this handout is adapted from *www. technologystudent.com/joints/hinge1.htm and www.dulley.com/diy/dw105. htm,* accessed April 16, 2008.)

Grass Type

Although a multitude of grass brands exists, there are basically two types of grasses: cool- and warm-season grasses, with each type better suited to particular climates in North America.

Cool-season grasses. These hardy grasses thrive in regions that experience cool or damp weather patterns. While these grasses tend to be quite resilient, they do not do well in hot, dry weather. During periods of extreme heat or aridity, cool-season grasses may turn brown or go dormant. They can be kept green by providing adequate hydration.

Warm-season grasses. These grasses are suited to hotter, dryer climates than are cool-season grasses. They do not require much maintenance and do better in poor soil conditions than do their cooler-weather counterparts. Another benefit of these grasses is that they offer an ideal environment for many types of wildlife. A major drawback is that they do not grow well in cooler climates and can experience a die-off during periods of cold weather. Patches of dead grass can be reseeded with cool-season grasses.

Transition zone grasses. There is a transition zone between northern and southern turf regions, which follows the lower elevations of Virginia and North Carolina west through West Virginia, Kentucky, Tennessee, and Arkansas. The transition zone includes southern Ohio, Indiana, Illinois, Missouri, and Kansas. In this transition zone, neither warm- nor cool-season grasses are uniformly successful. However, several of the northern, or cool-season, grasses, such as Kentucky bluegrass, perennial ryegrass, and tall fescue, do well across Kentucky, Virginia, West Virginia, and Missouri. Tall fescue is the best choice in Tennessee, North Carolina, northern Georgia, northern Alabama, and the Texas Panhandle. In the lower elevations of these latter states, warm-season grasses do well too.

Maintaining ideal growing conditions for your particular grass type is critical. Otherwise, unwanted grass varieties will pop up and will be extremely difficult to remove. For example, Saint Augustine grass invades Bermuda grass, and vice versa.

(The information about grasses on this handout is adapted from *www. american-lawns.com/grasses/grasses.html*, *www.allaboutlawns.com/ grass-types/cool-season-grasses.php*, and *www.sharpbro.com/clip010.htm*, accessed April 16, 2008.)

Criteria for Excellent Lessons

Effective catechists strive to present lessons that are . . .
- experiential
- participatory
- entertaining
- flexible
- multisensory
- incorporating multiple learning styles
- constructivist
- applicable
- welcoming
- safe
- prepared and organized
- dynamic
- innovative
- student-centered
- inclusive
- creative

Effective catechists strive to avoid lessons that are . . .
- boring
- repetitive
- unchallenging
- unimaginative
- typical
- disorganized
- passive
- sedentary
- rigid
- out of control
- overstructured
- teacher-centered
- uninspiring

9

Sowing the Seeds:
Dynamic Lesson Plans

What do you think? If a shepherd has a hundred sheep, and one of them has gone astray, does he not leave the ninety-nine on the mountains and go in search of the one that went astray? And if he finds it, truly I tell you, he rejoices over it more than over the ninety-nine that never went astray. So it is not the will of your Father in heaven that one of these little ones should be lost. (Matthew 18:12–14)

Together, let's look at the criteria described in chapters 7 and 8 to build an inclusive lesson plan based on the above parable of the last sheep. Examples will be provided, followed by space for you to add your own ideas.

Preparation

Gather the following items:

☐ handout 9–A, "Forgiveness," one for each student
☐ optional: music CD of the song "Forgiveness," by Jim Witter and Bobby Tomberlin, and a CD player
☐ a copy of lyrics that can be projected for one of the following or similar songs:
- "Shepherd Me, O God," by Marty Haugen
- "You Are Near," by Dan Schutte
- "Do Not Be Afraid," by Christopher Willcock

Activity A: Experiential Exercises

Remember that the student's experiences must be related to new information. As we connect the story to the experiences of the student's, we can look at this parable from three different perspectives: the lost sheep, the Good Shepherd, and the ninety-nine sheep left behind.

1. Being "Lost"

The first perspective is of the lost sheep. In your classroom you will have a range of concrete to abstract thinkers. Let's build two lists for each perspective to reflect both the literal and metaphorical experiences of being lost.

Ask yourself, What have all, or at least most, of the youth experienced that is similar to the experience of the lost sheep?

Concrete (Literal) Experiential Connections to Being Lost

- getting lost in a mall, a grocery store, or another public place
- losing your way on trails in a forest or park
- having trouble finding the correct route while driving in an unfamiliar neighborhood
- wandering off during a field trip or tour
- _____
- _____

Abstract (Metaphorical) Experiential Connections to Being Lost

- becoming confused during a math lesson
- being left out of a group of friends
- feeling distant from a close friend
- feeling separated from God
- _____
- _____

2. The Good Shepherd

The second perspective is that of the Good Shepherd. Again let's build two experiential lists, including both concrete and abstract thinkers.

Ask yourself, What have all, or at least most, of the youth experienced that is similar to the experience of the Good Shepherd?

Concrete (Literal) Experiential Connections to Finding the Lost Sheep

- helping a new student find the way on the first day of school
- stopping what you're doing to help a parent find the car keys
- giving directions to someone who is lost
- _____
- _____

Abstract (Metaphorical) Experiential Connections to Finding the Lost Sheep

- encouraging a friend to resist the temptation to do something wrong
- reaching out to a student who doesn't seem to have any friends
- giving up an evening out with friends to help a sibling with homework
- _____
- _____

3. The Other Ninety-Nine

The third perspective is that of the other ninety-nine sheep, who are left behind while the shepherd goes to search for the lost sheep. This perspective, like the elder son in the parable of the prodigal son, is often overlooked but contains rich insights into attitudes of siblings and peers toward youth with special needs. These people often feel left behind due to the extra attention the youth with special needs receives.

Ask yourself, What have all, or at least most, of the youth experienced that is similar to the experience of the sheep left behind?

Concrete (Literal) Experiential Connections to the Sheep Left Behind

- being left at home while your parent takes a sibling somewhere
- getting picked up late from an event, due to other family priorities
- missing a bus for a field trip
- _____
- _____

Abstract (Metaphorical) Experiential Connections to the Sheep Left Behind

- a sports game getting interrupted or cancelled due to a peer's injury
- a parent helping a sibling instead of you with homework
- a teacher spending more time with another student than with you
- _____
- _____

Now that we've built a good list of experiential connections, let's use some of them to create a few experiential exercises for the beginning of the lesson. Remember to use examples from both the concrete and the abstract lists to include all learners. Read over the following examples and then try to create your own experiential exercises.

4. Pulling the Wool Over Your Eyes

Begin this section by guiding your students in reflecting on their experiences of being lost. You can use the following script or develop your own:

○ Close your eyes and think back to the early days of your childhood. Try to remember a time when you got lost. If you cannot recall a time when you were lost, imagine what the experience might be like. Maybe it's in a grocery store, perhaps at the mall. Focus on your feelings at the time. How did you feel when you first realized you were lost? What emotions did you experience during the time you were lost? How did you feel when you were finally found?

5. Feeling a Little Sheepish

Invite your students to turn to a neighbor and talk about a time they felt lost. Maybe they felt confused during a class lesson, or perhaps they felt left out of an activity their friends were enjoying. Have your students ask their neighbors the following reflection questions. Write them on the board for visual learners:

• What happened that made you feel lost?
• What emotions did you experience?
• Did anyone rescue you? How did you feel when you were rescued? How did you feel if you were not rescued?

6. Shear Delight

Invite the students to think about a time when they rescued someone else who was lost. Explain that the stories can include both literal and figurative rescues, giving examples of each. Ask for volunteers to choose from the following options or come up with their own way to share the stories:

• The storyteller chooses two participants to act out the story while he or she is telling it aloud.
• The storyteller draws the story on the board with or without verbal sharing.
• The storyteller shares the story with one other person in the group, and that person relates the story to the large group.

7. Leaving Ewe Behind

Explore with the students their understandings and definitions of the word *fair*.

Invite two students to the front of the room to receive a treat. Use candy that comes in small pieces. Narrate as you give the candy to each participant: "I'm giving Jackie five pieces of candy, and I'm giving Oscar one piece." Look up, smile, and ask the students to return to their seats. Ask, "Was that fair?" Invite them to explain their answers. Then ask how they think you could have made it fairer.

Pose the following series of situations to the volunteers:
- What if Jackie (or Oscar) were allergic to chocolate?
- What if Oscar had already received four pieces of candy earlier?
- What if Oscar had already received six pieces of candy earlier?
- What if Jackie has OCD, and can eat candies only in groups of five?
- _____
- _____

Challenge the students by asking if circumstances change what is fair. Provide an alternative definition of *fairness* if the students do not: everybody gets what is needed, whether it is equal or not. Enjoy some dialogue with the young people about situations in which they felt left behind like the ninety-nine sheep. Explore the challenges of being neglected for a greater need.

Activity B: Creating a Participatory and Entertaining Lesson

There are many options for immersion in the content, in this case, the parable of the lost sheep. The scriptural passage could be read, or the story could be watched on a video, paraphrased in storytelling fashion, role-played, or performed. You could use puppets, costumes, and props to bring the story to life. The presentation is limited only by your imagination. As you create ideas for immersing the youth in the story, keep in mind that you want them to be involved in the learning, not passive recipients of information. Remember also to make the lesson captivating and entertaining.

1. Little Sheep of Horrors

Invite participants comfortable with spontaneous role-playing to assume one of the following parts:
- the Good Shepherd
- the lost sheep
- one of the ninety-nine sheep left behind (any number of participants can assume this role)

If you wish, use costumes and props to make the lesson more fun (a staff for the Good Shepherd, stick-on pieces of cotton for the sheep). Students may either take the stage or perform their parts from their seats. Instruct the students to provide spontaneous dialogue in the story, when prompted. Tell them it is okay to add humor but to keep it respectful and appropriate. Then in a lively, dramatic style, read (or better yet, tell) the story, pausing at the indicated places to prompt the role-players, using gestures such as a nod. Modify the gender of the pronouns, as needed, to match the volunteer for each role.

Once upon a time, there was a Good Shepherd, whose name was _____.
The Good Shepherd had one hundred wonderful sheep. He loved his sheep
so much that he was often heard to say, "_____." All the sheep loved
the Good Shepherd as well. They often praised him, saying things like
"_____," and "_____," and "_____." The sheep and the Good Shepherd were happy together.

Then one cold winter day, the Good Shepherd was counting the sheep,
and to his great horror, counted only ninety-nine in the flock! One of his
sheep was lost! He was upset and shouted, "_____!" There were many
different reactions in the rest of the flock. One of the ninety-nine said,
"_____." Another said, "_____." A third said, "_____."

The Good Shepherd left the ninety-nine sheep to go looking for the lost
sheep. As he disappeared in the distance, one of the ninety-nine whispered
to his friend, "_____."

The Good Shepherd searched and searched for the little lost sheep. Because he was determined to find the sheep and bring it back to the flock,
the Good Shepherd said, "_____."

Meanwhile the little lost sheep was all alone in an unfamiliar area. Feeling so alone and so lost, the sheep cried, "_____." He regretted having
wandered off from the rest of the flock. He hoped the Good Shepherd
would come to look for him. He called out to the Good Shepherd for help,
yelling, "_____!"

Back at the flock, some of the sheep were praying for the safe return
of the lost sheep. They prayed, "_____." Other sheep resented the lost
sheep. They missed the Good Shepherd and felt unsafe without him there.
One of these disgruntled sheep said, "Baaa, humbug," and complained,
"_____." Another whispered to his friend, "_____." A third shouted
out, "_____!" Those who were praying stopped and defended the Good
Shepherd's actions by saying, "_____." Another backed him up with,
"_____." The disgruntled sheep felt a little embarrassed. One even said,
"_____."

The lost sheep was cold, alone, and about to give up hope. He thought
he was a baaaaad sheep and didn't deserve to be rescued. He closed his
eyes, lowered his head, and cried softly to himself, "_____." He had never
felt so cold, so alone, so hopeless. *[Pause for effect.]*

[Loudly with excitement] But then something wonderful happened! The
sheep heard the most wonderful sound in the world. It was the sound
of his master's voice calling to him. He heard the Good Shepherd yell,
"_____!" The lost sheep shouted back, at the top of his lungs, "_____!"
The Good Shepherd came running up, scooped the sheep formerly known
as lost into his arms, and gave him the biggest, warmest hug he'd ever

experienced. The found sheep looked gratefully into the Good Shepherd's eyes and said, "_____."

The ninety-nine rejoiced when they saw the Good Shepherd crest the hill with their brother on his shoulders. The ninety-nine shouted all together, "_____!" The Good Shepherd smiled from ear to ear and shared his joy with the whole flock. He said, "_____." But the Good Shepherd knew that some of the flock had not been happy when he left the ninety-nine to go after the one. He explained to them why he did it, saying, "_____." The sheep understood and were glad their brother was back, safe and sound. One said, "_____." Another commented, "_____." A third warmly welcomed the formerly lost sheep back by saying, "_____."

And so the flock was restored. The Good Shepherd assured them all that if any were ever "on the lamb," he would search the neighborhood until they were found. "After all," he said, "You are all my kids . . . er . . . lambs."

2. Counting Sheep

To support the more concrete thinkers, follow up the role-play by soliciting identification of the symbols in the parable, including Jesus as the Good Shepherd, those who feel separated from Christ or community as the lost sheep, and the Body of Christ as the ninety-nine.

Activity C: Applying the Lesson to Real Life

Continue with an activity that reveals the parable's relevance to the lives of the students. Consider related events in the news that have occurred in the community or issues common to the youth in your area. Invite them to reflect silently on times in their lives when they may have strayed and how the Lord will always seek them out and accept them back into the flock. Emphasize that because the Lord is willing to take us back, we too should forgive others who have hurt us in our lives.

1. Bleating Hearts

1. Distribute copies of handout 9–A, "Forgiveness," which contains the lyrics for a contemporary Christian song related to the theme of reconciliation. Specifically it addresses the broken relationship between two friends, Mickey and Jim. Read the lyrics aloud or play the song on the CD player.

2. Follow the song with an activity in which you interview two volunteers taking on the roles of Mickey and Jim. This perspective-sharing role-play will

help those who have a difficult time seeing things from others' points of view, like those with autistic disorders.

Use the following questions for the interview and add a few of your own:

- Jim, what happened that caused you to end the friendship with Mickey?
- Jim, how did you feel when you found out Mickey had stolen your bike?
- Mickey, why did you steal Jim's bike?
- Mickey, when Jim asked you who stole the bike, why did you lie to him? How did you feel?
- Jim, which did you feel worse about: that Mickey stole the bike or that he lied to you about it? Explain your feelings.
- Mickey, years later, why did you decide to send Jim a card for his wedding? Why didn't you put your name on the card?
- Jim, when you received the card from Mickey, what did you think he was trying to do? Why didn't you respond to the card?
- Mickey, how did you feel when Jim didn't respond?
- Jim, describe your thoughts and feelings when you read in the paper that Mickey had died.
- Mickey, if you had it to do all over again, what would you do differently?
- Jim, if you had it to do all over again, how would you change the story?
- Mickey, now that Jim is here, is there something you'd like to say to him?
- Jim, would you like to respond to Mickey?

3. Thank the participants who played the roles and ask them to return to the large group.

2. Taking Stock of the Flock

1. Extend the interview by asking the following questions of the large group, at the same time writing them on the board. Ask the students not to respond aloud but to either answer on paper or just think about their answers.

- If you had been Mickey, what would you have done?
- If you had been Jim, would you change the way you reacted?
- Have you ever been separated from friends or family members because of a hurtful event like this one?
- Would you be open to trying to reconcile and heal the relationship?
- What first step could you take to forgive or ask for forgiveness?
- _____
- _____

2. Invite the students to write a letter (provide keyboard or scribe options for those with trouble writing), taking the role of either Mickey or Jim. Encourage them to take ownership and apologize for any wrongdoing their characters may have done and to forgive any wrongdoing the other person may have done. Invite a few students (from both Mickey's and Jim's perspectives) to read their letters aloud. Close by encouraging the students to reflect on their own lives and relationships and to pursue reconciliation with those they have hurt or been hurt by.

Activity D: Closing Prayer

To close the lessons, sing together one of the following songs, or a similar song, with lyrics printed, projected, or written on the board:
- "Shepherd Me, O God," by Marty Haugen
- "You Are Near," by Dan Schutte
- "Do Not Be Afraid," by Christopher Willcock

Tell the participants the group will pause between verses for spontaneous prayer centered on the theme of reconciliation. Give examples of prayer forms the participants might use, such as prayers of petition, praise, and thanksgiving.

Activity E: Further Review

Go back through this lesson plan, asking yourself the following questions based on the criteria presented in chapters 7 and 8. Modify the lesson to meet the needs of the students.

Is the lesson . . .
- experiential?
- participatory?
- entertaining?
- flexible?
- multisensory, incorporating different learning styles and multiple intelligences?
- constructivist?
- applicable to real life?
- student centered?
- innovative?

Now that you have walked through this process, you can use it to modify existing curriculums to include these features and enhance the catechetical experience for all your students.

Forgiveness

by Jim Witter and Bobby Tomberlin

Little Mickey Johnson was my very best friend
In first grade we swore we'd stay that way to the end
But in seventh grade somebody stole my bike
I asked Mickey if he knew who did it, and he lied
Cause it was him . . .
And when I found out it hit me like a ton of bricks
And I can still see that look on his face when I said
"I never want to talk to you again"
Sometimes we lose our way
We don't say things we should say
We hold on to stubborn pride
When we should put it all aside
To waste the time we're given seems so senseless
And one little word shouldn't be so hard . . .
Forgiveness . . .
A little card arrived on my wedding day
"Best wishes from an old friend" was all it had to say
No return address, no, not even a name
But the messy way that it was written gave it away
It was him . . .
And I just had to laugh as the past came flooding through my mind
I should have picked up that phone right then and there
But I just didn't make the time . . .
Sometimes we lose our way
We don't say things we should say
We hold on to stubborn pride
When we should put it all aside
To waste the time we're given seems so senseless
And one little word shouldn't be so hard . . .
Forgiveness . . .
Sunday morning paper arrived on my step
The first thing I read filled my heart with regret
I saw a name I hadn't seen in a while
It said he was survived by a wife and a child
And it was him . . .
When I found out, the tears just fell like rain
Cause I realized that I'd missed my chance

To ever talk to him again . . .
Sometimes we lose our way
We don't say things we should say
We hold on to stubborn pride
When we should put it all aside
To waste the time we're given seems so senseless
And one little word shouldn't be so hard . . .
Forgiveness . . .
One little word shouldn't be so hard . . .
Little Mickey Johnson was my very best friend . . .

[The lyrics on this handout are from the song "Forgiveness" by Jim Witter and Bobby Tomberlin, on the album *Forgiveness,* (Curb Records, 2003). Used with permission of Mike Curb Music (BMI)/Curb Songs (ASCAP).]

10

Nourishing the Crops: Classroom Management

What do you think is the most challenging aspect of serving as a volunteer catechist? Is it the time commitment? understanding the material? presenting the lessons?

In reality, each of these may be a cakewalk compared with the challenges of classroom management and discipline. Volunteers often enter the religious education classroom with little or no training in this area, armed only with the memory of their own experiences of discipline from their youth. When confronted with behavior issues, catechists may deal with them in ways that do not promote growth and learning. When managing students in a classroom, it is often the counterintuitive response, doing the opposite of what comes naturally, that is best for the young person.

What Is Discipline?

Our understanding of discipline affects how it occurs in the classroom. Often discipline is equated with punishment. Many of us grew up with adults who used punishment as the primary tool in response to behavior that was not appropriate. In punitive models the adult sets the rules, and when the young people behave in ways inconsistent with the expectations of the rules, the adult judges the behavior and enforces the rules by delivering unpleasant consequences. The practice assumes that the unpleasant consequences will extinguish the behavior in the future. Punitive models are based on adults' using their power to control the actions of the young people. Using a punitive parenting model, for example, the parents determine and communicate the rules, such as "Don't jump on the bed." If a child breaks the rule and is caught jumping on the bed, the parent then delivers a punishment. This could range from a spanking to a loss of some privilege.

Punitive models are sometimes criticized for their harshness. There is often a greater harm. Adults who use punishment as their only disciplinary tool are robbing the young people of the ability to own their behavior. Ownership of behavior means taking personal responsibility, being in charge of one's interactions with others. Using the ownership model, all discipline is self-discipline. The parent or teacher acts as a guide or facilitator, but the young people, to the degree they are developmentally able, are responsible for the problem solving necessary to resolve the issue, as well as making restitution for any harm caused.

Johnny Jumps on the Bed

Let's compare the two discipline styles in the case of Johnny jumping on the bed. Let's say Johnny is a typically developing seven-year-old. Dad has just walked into the bedroom and discovered Johnny gleefully jumping on the bed. In a punitive approach, the interaction might go something like this:

> **Dad [in an angry voice]:**   Johnny, get down from there right now! I told you the rule about no jumping on the beds. Because you broke this rule, you won't be getting any dessert after dinner. Don't you ever jump on the bed again!

Using this model Dad has full ownership of the interaction. Dad sets the rule and decides the punishment. Johnny does not get an opportunity to problem-solve or to practice taking responsibility for his behavior. The assumption in the house is that rules should never be broken and when they are, it is Dad's job to fix it, using negative reinforcement.

Using a model in which Johnny has more ownership, Dad assumes the role of coach or facilitator, and the goal shifts to providing opportunities for Johnny to practice. The assumption in this house is that rules will be broken, that everyone makes not-so-good choices now and then, and when this happens, the person making the mistake is responsible for problem solving, clearing up any miscommunication, and making restitution if harm has been done. In a home in which young people have ownership, the interaction might go something like this:

> *Dad walks into the room where Johnny is jumping on the bed. Johnny immediately stops and climbs down.*
> **Dad [with a neutral tone and calm affect]:**   What's happening, Johnny?
> **Johnny:**   I was jumping on the bed.
> **Dad:**   Yeah, I noticed that. What do you think about that?
> **Johnny:**   I shouldn't do it.
> **Dad:**   I think that's right. Why? Do you remember what we talked about at the family meeting when we agreed not to do that?
> **Johnny:**   Because it could break, or I could get hurt.
> **Dad:**   That's right. But you looked like you were having a lot of fun up there.

Johnny: I was!

Dad: So how could you have that kind of fun without risking the furniture or your bones?

Johnny: Um . . . *[thinking it through]* Well, my friend, Riley, has a trampoline in his backyard. *[big smile]* Could we get a trampoline?!

Dad: Sure it's a possibility. If you want, we can look on the Internet after supper. I can help you get some prices and make a plan for doing extra chores to earn the money to pay for it.

Johnny: That would be great, Dad! And I'm sorry I jumped on the bed.

Dad: That's great, Johnny. Now let's go eat.

In this scenario Dad is not the enforcer or the controller. His goal is to support Johnny in his coordination with the rest of the family and to coach Johnny as he thinks through his actions and motivations. Dad also recognizes that there is a good desire at the root of the choice. Johnny likes to jump. Dad coaches Johnny toward making better choices to meet Johnny's needs.

Your first reaction to this scenario might be that this scene is an unrealistic fantasy, that in the real world, things don't go this smoothly. That's true because, typically, the adult does not consider the positive motivation behind the negative behavior. The assumption that drives typical disciplinary styles is this: "Kids want to do the wrong thing, and it is the adult's job to influence them to do the right thing." We at The Monarch School believe young people want to do the right thing, and when treated with care and respect, they typically work hard to do the right thing. Conversations like the second one between Jonnny and his father, although it sounds too good to be true, happen every day at Monarch. That is not to say it is always easy. Problem solving can be hard and time-consuming work. But the question of discipline really boils down to who will do this work.

It's fascinating to compare the following definitions and understandings of the word *discipline*, with its root, *disciple*:

dis·ci·pline

1. To train by instruction and practice, especially to teach self-control to.

2. To teach to obey rules or accept authority. . . .

3. To punish in order to gain control or enforce obedience. . . .

4. To impose order on: *needed to discipline their study habits.*

(The American Heritage Dictionary of the English Language, fourth edition)

dis·cip·le

1a. One who embraces and assists in spreading the teachings of another.

1b. An active adherent, as of a movement or philosophy.

2. often **Disciple:** One of the original followers of Jesus. . . .

(The American Heritage Dictionary of the English Language, fourth edition)

As you consider each definition, do you see the contradiction between *discipline* and *disciple*?

The role of disciple by definition is proactive: to take personal responsibility to learn and follow the teachings of a master. The master's responsibility is not to control or compel the disciple. But many people feel it is the parent's job to discipline a child; that it is the teacher's job to discipline a student, as opposed to the student being responsible for her or his own discipline.

Consider the following questions:

- Who is responsible for student behavior in the classroom?
- Whose job is it to ensure that students behave in a manner that promotes good learning?
- When students behave in inappropriate ways, who should be responsible for making a plan to improve?

How we answer these questions has a profound effect on the development of the young people in our charge.

Jesus and Discipline

The Gospels make it clear that Jesus' view of discipline places the ownership and responsibility for the learning with the follower rather than with himself. He took the role of teacher, to be sure, but didn't take responsibility for his followers' compliance. One of the best illustrations of this belief and practice in the Scriptures is the parable of Jesus and the rich man:

> A certain ruler asked him, "Good Teacher, what must I do to inherit eternal life?" Jesus said to him, "Why do you call me good? No one is good but God alone. You know the commandments: 'You shall not commit adultery; You shall not murder; You shall not steal; You shall not bear false witness; Honor your father and mother.'" He replied, "I have kept all these since my youth." When Jesus heard this, he said to him, "There is still one thing lacking. Sell all that you own and distribute the money to the poor, and you will have treasure in heaven; then come, follow me." But when he heard this, he became sad; for he was very rich. Jesus looked at him and said, "How hard it is for those who have wealth to enter the kingdom of God! Indeed, it is easier for a camel to go through the eye of a needle than for someone who is rich to enter the kingdom of God." Those who heard it said, "Then who can be saved?" He replied, "What is impossible for mortals is possible for God." (Luke 18:18–27)

Jesus clearly fulfills his role as teacher here but does not try to exert his power to control the rich man's response. Jesus provides the man with guidance but does not compel his acceptance. He allows the rich man to own his own development. The master doesn't chase him. He lets the man go. He understands that the rich man is not developmentally ready to take the next step in faith, to allow God to help him. Jesus doesn't carry him to a place he is not ready to go.

Footprints in the Sand

In this inspirational story, a man dreams he is walking along the beach with the Lord, and he sees scenes from his life flash across the sky. For each scene, he sees two sets of footprints in the sand, one belonging to him, and the other to the Lord. When he reaches the end of the journey, he looks back and notices that at the worst times in his life, there was only one set of footprints. He questions the Lord, thinking Jesus had abandoned him during those hard times. The Lord reassures the man there is only one set of footprints because, during those times of trial, it was then that the Lord carried him.

The tender care of the Lord in this story is touching, but the brilliance of the story is the balance with which the Lord accompanies the man throughout his life. Jesus doesn't carry him through all the bad times in his life, only the worst ones. The Lord carries the man only when he can't walk on his own. How would the man's life have been different if the Lord had carried him through all the times of struggle? How would his journey have been different if the Lord had never carried him?

Ownership in the Classroom

In imitation of Jesus, effective catechists provide the guidance, support, and encouragement young people need to grow, and allow them to own their own behavior and development. Students experience the most success when the adults in their lives allow them to walk on their own to the degree they are able, carrying them only when they are developmentally not capable. Consider how difficult it would be for infants to learn to walk if their parents scooped them up and carried them every time they tried to take a few steps. With caring intentions catechists may be inclined to carry students who have special needs, doing things for them that the students could, with struggle, accomplish on their own.

Let's take, for example, the case of Ruth. She is a student who often loses focus on the lesson and instead stares out the window. If the catechist takes complete ownership of the problem and frequently calls out Ruth's name to get her to focus, the catechist is carrying Ruth. If Ruth owns her attention difference, it is up to her, with the catechist acting as coach, to set goals and plan to improve her ability to focus.

The challenge is to find just the right balance of teacher ownership and student ownership, based on the age of typically developing students. What is likely to happen if you ask a two-year-old child to fix a peanut-butter-and-jelly sandwich? Would the child be successful? The child would likely succeed at making a big mess. Why? Because the cognitive, spatial, and fine-motor skills of a child at age two are typically not advanced enough to complete the task successfully. This is an appropriate time to carry the child by making the sandwich for the child.

As the child grows developmentally, she or he becomes more capable and should gradually be allowed more ownership. Continuing with the example of the peanut-butter-and-jelly sandwich, what could a typically developing three-year-old contribute to the process? Clearly the child is not ready to assume full ownership of the lunch preparation, but can the child own part of it? Absolutely. She or he can make choices: chunky or smooth. The child could hold the bread while you spread the peanut butter. As the child grows, more and more responsibility should shift from the adult to the child until the child is capable of fully owning the process.

Ownership and Special Needs

In the previous example, chronological ages were used to designate developmental levels. Notice that *age* was modified by *typically developing*. This is because, although rare, some two-year-olds would have no problem successfully making a peanut-butter-and-jelly sandwich. Additionally some teens are not developmentally capable of performing this task successfully.

In application to classroom management, catechists enter a classroom with certain expectations of behavior based on chronological groupings. Teachers expect different behaviors from a class of elementary students compared with a class of high school students. Generally speaking, this is reliable. But when considering special needs, it is crucial to modify expectations not on chronological age but rather on the developmental characteristics of each student.

For example, when young people don't get what they want, they can experience emotional upset. The degree to which they can regulate their emotions varies developmentally. In early childhood crying, screaming, and kicking are common reactions. In adolescence these behaviors can still occur but are less likely. In all classrooms the students' developmental level of self-regulation skills varies, and those with special needs may exhibit behaviors more common to younger children.

Using a chronological frame, temper tantrums exhibited by teenagers, complete with crying and screaming, may be judged as infantile behavior, causing an impulse to shame the students. The catechist may react with a classroom management approach that is hurtful, implying or even verbalizing an expectation that the teens get control of themselves or act their ages.

Using a developmental frame, the catechist would understand that even though the students are teens, their levels of self-regulation are such that they cannot always control or regulate those feelings of upset. This includes recognition that the students' levels of ownership of self-regulation are low. So the reaction is likely to be less judgmental, more understanding, and more supportive. Understanding the developmental level will create in the catechist an impulse to provide understanding and comfort to the students, with comments like: "I see you're very upset. Do you want to use the break area to take a break and calm down?"

In skills that affect their student's behaviors in the classroom, any given chronological grouping will contain a wide spectrum of developmental levels, regardless of whether the students are in a group with specifically identified special needs. So in a middle school catechetical group of ages 11 to 13, there may be a developmental span of 5 to 7 years, with some youth functioning below typically developing youth and some functioning above.

The best approach for the catechist is to accept all students for who, what, and where they are developmentally, regardless of their chronological ages, and to support them in their efforts to grow with the right balance of youth and catechist ownership of their classroom behaviors. Students should be expected to own their behaviors based not on their chronological ages but on their developmental levels.

The Danger of Extremes

A former Monarch student who has been diagnosed with Asperger's syndrome, an autistic spectrum disorder characterized by advanced language skills with significant social differences, shared his struggle in school before coming to Monarch:

> My teachers just didn't understand me. Some of them, when they found out I had Asperger's, would treat me like a baby. I have an IQ over 140. I'm not retarded. They talked to me like you would a five-year-old, doing everything for me. And no matter what I did, they'd say, "That's okay, you can't help it." It was so condescending.

This student was frustrated with the low level of ownership afforded him. With other teachers the level of ownership afforded was too high:

> Some teachers didn't understand my Asperger's. They expected me to be just like the other kids, and when I got in fights with my classmates, the teacher wouldn't help me. She'd just say, "You're old enough to work that out on your own." Everybody hated me.

An expectation of ownership that is too high or too low can torpedo student development.

How does a catechist discern the appropriate balance of youth and adult ownership?

Getting It Right

This may seem overwhelming, but with the right combination of registration information, parent input, consistent classroom structure, and direct contact with each young person, catechists can know their students well enough to recognize the appropriate levels of ownership in the different areas of their students' development. It's crucial to recognize that developmental growth is a dynamic process. The key is openness to adjustment based on these interactions as catechists get to know the youth better. Nobody gets it perfect every time.

For example, you may have on your roster a student—let's call him Frank.

Step One: Look at the Registration Materials

Frank's parent included on his registration that he has trouble processing auditory information. This gives you a basic understanding of Frank's learning difference, but it doesn't tell you anything about Frank's history, level of ownership, ability to make accommodations on his own, and so on.

Step Two: Talk with the Parent

To learn more you talk with Frank's mother on the phone. She tells you Frank is a slow processor of information communicated verbally. In the past this has resulted in Frank's getting bored and acting out in the classroom. She shares that Frank is aware of his learning difference and has developed a strategy in school that has been helpful. She tells you he jots down key words throughout the lesson and also tape-records the lessons and uses the recording to fill in the gaps later. After this conversation you feel you better understand Frank's learning difference.

Step Three: Interact with the Student in the Classroom

On the first day of class, Frank sits in the front row, but you don't see a tape recorder. Class begins, and still no recorder. Throughout the first half of the lesson, Frank cracks jokes, interrupts, and makes inappropriate comments. You are curious about what's happening.

Step Four: Coach the Student

In the role of coach, you approach Frank during a break and chat a little bit as follows:

Catechist: Frank, your mom shared that you sometimes jot down notes and use a tape recorder to help you get all the information spoken in the classroom.

Frank: Yeah, but I forgot it at home.

Catechist: Do you usually remember to bring the recorder?

Frank: Sometimes.

Catechist: *[thinks: "Frank is teaching me that he not only has a processing difference, but he also struggles in the executive function of organization." The catechist, recognizing that the student needs to practice the skill of remembering to bring necessary tools, coaches in that direction.]* Do you have any ideas for ways to remember to bring it?

Frank: I could just try to remember.

Catechist: Has that worked in the past?

Frank: Not really.

Catechist: What else could you try?

Frank: Well, I could ask my mom to remind me.

Catechist: *[thinks: "I don't really know Frank's level of ownership here. Mom's prompts might be carrying Frank, or it might be the appropriate level of intervention as a step toward Frank's remembering on his own. I'll probe a little bit more to see what I can find out.]* Have you tried anything else to help you remember?

Frank: We used to have a checklist.

Catechist: Tell me about that.

Frank: Well, it would have all the stuff I needed to remember to do before leaving, and we'd put it on the door so I couldn't leave without seeing it. Then I'd check off all the stuff before I left.

Catechist: How did that work?

Frank: Good.

Catechist: Are you still using it?

Frank: For school, yes.

Catechist: Do you think you could add bringing your tape recorder here to your list and check it before leaving for class?

Frank: Sure.

Catechist: Great. Let's give that a try.

Step Five: Observe and Reflect

The catechist understands that Frank's acting out is a result of his processing difference. She watches for the next few weeks to see if Frank remembers and uses his recorder, takes notes, or acts out. She coaches him again, celebrating his success if it works and guiding him through the process of reflecting on the experiment, possibly tweaking it to make it more effective or trying something completely different if it's not working. But it's Frank doing the work, Frank setting the goals, Frank running the experiments, and Frank reflecting on his progress. Frank owns his neurological differences.

The Many Faces of Ownership

Who will own the classroom management and discipline in your classrooms? Both teachers and students should own this work, with students doing as much as they are developmentally able. But what do discipline and classroom management look like when the students own them? It might be helpful to consider the following dichotomy when designing classroom structure and training catechists.

Catechist- or Student-Generated Shared Values?

It is difficult to own rules imposed on us from outside. The students who participate in the creation of shared values, procedures, and expectations for respectful behavior are more likely to internalize and practice them. A good way to do this and be sure to include everything necessary is to provide students with categories, such as using language in class, and ask them to design the standard for appropriate behavior, such as "Students and catechists will speak to each other with respect, using only appropriate language in a respectful tone."

Following is a suggested list of categories for shared values generation:
- arrival and dismissal procedures
- participation
- movement in and around the classroom
- use of signals for attention
- use and care of books and supplies
- timeliness
- attitude
- respectful disagreements
- use of restrooms
- confidentiality
- cleanup procedures
- overall respect

Catechist- or Student-Defended Values?

If the catechist is the only one who speaks up when the values are threatened, then that person is the only one who owns the values. This creates an "us versus them" climate and often puts the catechist in an adversarial role with the students. Students who have the ability to respectfully defend the values of the community in the classroom are more likely themselves to demonstrate those values. This can be messy, because there is a risk of students tattling or embarrassing one another. It is important that time be spent discussing and deciding ways to defend the values that respect others.

Catechist Directives or Student Choices?

When students make positive evaluations and choices for their own development, they increase their ownership. When a catechist decides and issues directives to students, the students are less likely to be able to make that choice for themselves in other instances.

Following is an example of a directive approach when a student is distracted:

Catechist: Kim, you are distracted. Go and get a soother from the soother station.

Following is an example of a student-owned evaluation and choice:

Catechist: Kim, what's happening?
Kim: I'm having a hard time staying focused.
Catechist: What do you want to do?
Kim: I could get a soother.
Catechist: Great idea.

In both cases the catechist is involved, but the role is different. In the first example, the catechist takes an authoritarian role, so Kim has no opportunity to take ownership. In the second example, the catechist takes the role of coach, giving prompts that help Kim increase her ownership in paying attention. The second approach will help Kim prepare to self-manage in other settings or when the catechist is not focused on her.

Rigidity or Flexibility?

Do students have the opportunity to ask for exceptions to the rules or lesson plans based on individual needs and abilities? When students resist complying with a catechist's request, there is usually a good reason, and it is often developmentally based. For example, the lesson plans may ask for students to share in groups of six. Some students are not developmentally capable of successfully coordinating with that many people. If they complain, resist sharing, or get disruptive whenever small groups are formed, their behavior may communicate that an exception needs to be made. In this case it is easy to allow smaller groupings for sharing, or even simply to write down the response individually as an alternative. An open environment in which compliance is not compulsory increases student ownership and ultimately improves order and calm in the classroom.

Judgment or Curiosity?

When students demonstrate disruptive or inappropriate behavior, what typically pops into the teacher's head? Thoughts might include, This student is being disrespectful or This student is challenging my authority. These thoughts can be quickly followed by a snap judgment of the behavior and a sharp response. Instead, a teacher should stop and consciously decide to be curious, internally wondering, What might be happening? What is this student trying to teach me? What is the behavior telling me? What experiments could I run in response? Curiosity preserves the dignity and increases the ownership the student holds.

Consider a classroom situation in which a student snaps a pencil in half. Reactive leaps to judgment, such as thinking the student chose to disrespect property, usually completely miss the mark. Any given behavior could have many different causes, and confronting a student with an impulsive judgment most often makes the situation worse. In the case of the broken pencil, the following are some things that might be going on with the student:

- He needs to move. He has been sitting in his place too long. He's at the end of his attention span.
- She is having problems interacting with another student and feels angry or frustrated about it.
- He is thinking about a heated disagreement he had with his father on the way to class.
- She has difficulty writing and has accidentally broken the pencil.
- He has difficulty writing and has broken the pencil because he is frustrated.
- She accidentally broke the pencil.

The list could go on and on. Immediately correcting the student will likely result in anger or alienation from the group for the remainder of the class period. Curiosity, gentle questioning, and reflection could result in a greater understanding of the student's needs.

Willful or Developmental Frame?

When encountering inappropriate behavior, does the catechist interpret the behavior as willful or developmentally based? Is the behavior described objectively or with character-laden adjectives (*bad, misbehaving, disruptive*)? Regardless of whether the behavior is willful, a developmental approach is a more effective way to problem-solve and is more likely to encourage student growth. Willful interpretations and responses are more likely to provoke oppositional behavior or leave the student feeling powerless and shamed.

Problems as Aberration or Integral?

Does the catechist react to behavior problems as if they should never occur and as if they constitute crises? or does the catechist see them as expected and welcome parts of developmental growth? It is difficult for students to take ownership of their own development when missteps are interpreted as not belonging. If problems are seen as opportunities to practice, as opposed to failures, students are much more likely to work on them.

Doing the Right Thing

Ultimately we at The Monarch School believe young people want to do the right thing, want to learn, want to get along well with others, want to be organized and prepared, and want to be in charge of their own development. When students aren't successful in these pursuits, our job is not to force their compliance. We see the adult role as guide, coach, and mentor, to support the students by suspending judgment, being curious, running experiments, and providing many opportunities for practice. We have seen the fruits of this empowering approach in students who grow to become independent, self-reliant, and successful in their learning!

11

Crop Report

The report is in, and the news is good! How exciting to see more dioceses addressing the issue of including youth with special needs! As your community moves forward in making changes that respect the needs of all the youth, know that you are not alone. In 2007 we at The Monarch School conducted a survey of diocesan directors of religious education (DREs) from around the country to determine what they were doing to assist youth with special needs in religious education programs. We contacted all 189 U.S. dioceses and received responses from 159. In the survey we simply asked the two following questions:

1. Do the religious education programs for youth in your parishes include any special modifications or accommodations for youth with special needs?
2. Do your parish directors of education or your catechists receive any special training for working with youth with special needs?

In response to the first question, 97, or 61 percent, responded yes, they do indeed provide modifications.

In response to the second question, 59, or 37 percent, shared that they provide training for DREs and catechists in working with youth with special needs. Chart 11–A shows the results in graphic form.

Chart 11-A Diocesan Survey Resume

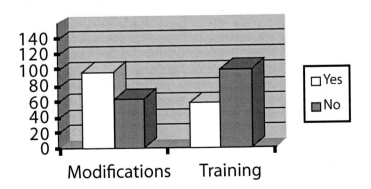

The Need

One positive finding of our survey is that the majority of DREs understand the need for accommodations and modifications for youth with special needs in religious education programs. Several comments we received as part of the survey expressed this growing reality.

Deacon Dan Hannig, director of faith formation for the Diocese of Crookston, Minnesota, states it this way: "There is certainly a need to provide more and better material on this topic."

Yvonne Harrold, director of special education for the Diocese of Stockton, California, demonstrates her recognition of the need with a strong policy of inclusion: "I *always* include the children in a regular classroom. I think that's very important so they know they are like everyone else in the eyes of God, whether they have a disability or not."

Rebecca Titford, director of the office of religious education for the Archdiocese of Mobile, Alabama, tells us: "Most of the parishes would do anything to help, if asked—they all have very inclusive attitudes. This particular group of parents and students is hard to get a handle on. They often won't identify themselves to us; they're a very silent, underrepresented group."

The Rising Urgency

Before we delve into more findings of the survey, we must address one other statistic. It is clear that there is an increasing population of diagnosed cases of neurological differences. Chart 11–B vividly demonstrates the rising national rates of autism, which some researchers and epidemiologists are calling the autism epidemic.

1990: "[Autism] occurs in one to two out of every 1,000 births [and] . . . is distributed throughout the world among all races, nationalities, and social classes." (Division TEACCH Web site)

1993: "Autism is one of the four major developmental disabilities. It occurs in one to two of every 1,000 births." (Division TEACCH Web site)

2000: "Average . . . prevalence [of autism] was 6.7 per 1,000 children aged 8 years." (Centers for Disease Control and Prevention Web site)

2007: Prevalence rates have been placed at 1 in every 150 children, one out of every 94 male births. (Centers for Disease Control and Prevention Web site)

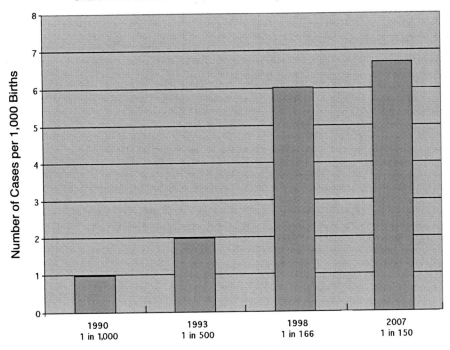

Chart 11-B: Incidence Rates of Autism per 1,000 Births

The Responsibility

In recognizing this rising trend of diagnosed neurological differences in youth, parishes and dioceses must take on greater responsibility in developing religious education programs that address the needs of all participants.
As part of this, the development of resources to assist parishes and parishioners in understanding the needs of youth with special needs and how to serve them is critical.

According to Anne Masters, director of pastoral ministries in the Archdiocese of Newark, New Jersey: "There is enhanced sensitivity now, so there are more parishes who are trying to reach out. So even on the archdiocesan level, we are also trying to reach out to parents and let them know there is a need, and to be proactive."

Although Masters shows remarkable sensitivity to this issue, she acknowledges the challenges in meeting the need throughout the archdiocese:

> It really runs the gamut in terms of what is being done. There are some programs that have been running for twenty years, and there are some that are just trying to figure it out, and there are some that are still not even wanting to return the phone call from parents [who call to ask about

religious education for their children with special needs]. The ones that have been going for a while tend to become something like centers, and they take in children from other parishes. Those have a separate program, but even in those places they try to include them in regular classes when appropriate.

We found this to be a recurrent theme throughout other dioceses as well, with a great disparity of offerings in different parishes for different reasons, including financial constraints, geographical distance between parishes and families, difficulty finding resources, and lack of awareness.

Sr. Julie O'Neill, coordinator of special needs for religious education and youth ministry in the Diocese of San Francisco, shared: "We leave it up to the parishes to decide whether they feel they are able to serve those kids. Since only a few of the larger parishes have these resources, parents must decide if they are willing to travel outside of their home parish to make sure their child receives a religious education."

Sr. Margaret Kuntz, ASCJ, director for Christian formation for the Diocese of Pensacola-Tallahassee, Florida, told us that, although she realizes there is probably a need for special programs and services for youth with special needs, her diocese has trouble accessing what little material is available. Like several other religious education directors we spoke with, Kuntz said she was not aware of many families in her diocese that would require such services. When asked whether she thought the families weren't there or just weren't participating in the programs, she said, "I think it's a little bit of both."

Sr. Mary Dumonceaux, OSF, associate director of the Archdiocesan Catechetical Center (ACC) for the Diocese of San Antonio, Texas, told us: "A committee to advocate for catechesis for persons with disabilities meets on a regular basis. We are preparing samples of materials and lesson plans used for catechesis with these groups since a national search revealed a lack of available resources."

Bright Spots

Our survey confirmed what we already believed: leaders in the Church care about and want to include all youth in their programs, and it is challenging to provide for the needs of everyone. Following are some strategies for meeting the challenge, along with remarkable cases of diocesan and archdiocesan leaders who have risen to the challenge and provided innovative care for the youth in their religious education programs.

Family-Centered Programs and Special Education Curriculum

Linda Porter, director of faith formation for the Diocese of Tyler, Texas, provides a religious education curriculum that focuses on doctrines of faith, with revisions, suggestions, and modifications for use with special needs students. The diocese is moving toward a more family-oriented, or "lifespan," approach to religious education. With this shift to a more community-based approach to religious education, the diocese has seen many more people from all ages and groups come forward. "Last year we revised our curriculum guide and added a special education section to the end of it, including resources for the student," Porter said. "We're moving in the direction of family catechesis, which is more inclusive for special needs students and their families."

This community-centered approach also extends to sacramental preparation, in which parents are welcome to accompany their children to classes. Porter added:

> We find that more families who have children with special needs enroll their kids in sacrament preparation when they are allowed to come with them. We also have older adults with special needs who have enrolled in sacrament preparation and catechesis now, whereas they wouldn't do it before because they were not included as children, or they were scared or didn't feel welcome.

Contacts with Special Education Professionals

Thanks to its efforts to partner with special needs professionals, the Archdiocese of Newark is taking huge steps to enhance awareness among its parishes.

"We are very fortunate here," shared Anne Masters. "We have several special education professionals who are members of our diocese, and they have done a lot in terms of helping us take the strategies that are used in regular education and apply them to religious education and developing catechist training."

The Diocese of Austin, Texas, employs the same strategy. "What we try to do in RE [religious education] programs [for special needs youth] is to mainstream them as much as possible," shared Dr. Geri Telepak, director of religious education and formation, "and we are blessed that in many of our parishes we have special education teachers who volunteer, and who often serve as aides in the classroom rather than as teachers for the whole class."

Workshops and Resource Materials

Another useful strategy some dioceses employ is the development of workshops and resource materials addressing catechesis for youth with special needs.

Elizabeth Field, DRE for the Diocese of Camden, New Jersey, shared the following:

> Last June, our office, in collaboration with the Hispanic Ministry Office, offered a workshop on diversity that was divided into ways to address Hispanic children and children with special needs. We had speakers on both topics. This year I have ordered two pamphlets for all the PCLs [parish catechetical leaders] on understanding and assisting children and adults with special needs to learn their faith. We also are planning a follow-up to last June.

Training Integrated into Certification

Some dioceses have gone the extra mile in integrating special needs instruction as a requirement to be certified as a catechist in the diocese. Marsha Rivas, director of the Office of Equal Access Ministry for the Diocese of Toledo, Ohio, told us: "We offer special training specifically for learning disabilities, ADHD, and autism. We have included learning differences as a required part of the certification program."

Flexibility with Requirements

Many programs recognize that a one-size-fits-all approach to catechesis can result in some youth being left out. Churches are becoming more flexible about their requirements. "Special allowances are made in our sacrament preparation classes for youth with special needs," shared Yvonne Harrold, director of special education for the Diocese of Stockton. "They receive the sacrament like everyone else does, but we waive things they are not capable of, such as community service or retreats that might be too intense for them."

Direct Communication with Parents

It is encouraging to see many recognizing that open communication is an integral part of serving youth with special needs. In the Diocese of Stockton, they are committed to keeping the lines of communication open. "I talk to parents," said Harrold, "to find out the extent of the disability and what their child is capable of."

Accommodations and Modifications

Quite a few dioceses have advanced to the point where they have integrated special accommodations and modifications. Charleen Katra, associate director of continuing Christian education in the Archdiocese of Galveston-Houston, shared that most parishes in the diocese offer modifications, including pairing with other students in a buddy system, offering a break area, and adapting materials in response to the differing needs of the participants. Doreen Engel, director of spiritual education for the Archdiocese of Washington, D.C., also lists options available in her diocese to youth with special needs:

- priority scheduling—Parents of children with special needs can choose the type or session most comfortable for their children. This is especially important for youth on medication.
- in-class assistant—Children can be with their peers but still get the one-on-one help they need.
- partial classroom placement—Children may be in the regular classroom for the introduction to the lesson and then leave the room to work in a smaller group.
- one-on-one instruction—When necessary, students may have their own individual instructors.

Wonderful Responses, More to Do

Our research and our experiences at The Monarch School clearly show wonderful steps being taken by dioceses and parishes to serve the youth with special needs in their religious education programs. One thing that became clear to us in the survey is that no single response is ideal for every community. The diversity of responses and steps taken show that dioceses have selected a variety of paths to achieve the same goal. Much still must be done to meet the needs of youth with neurological differences. The most important thing, though, is that efforts are being made and will continue to develop as dioceses see the fruits of their hard work.

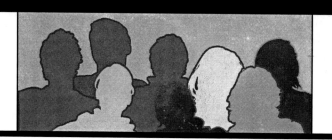

12

Reaping the Harvest

We at The Monarch School would like to thank you for reading this book. In doing so you have taken the first step in developing or enhancing a religious education and youth ministry program that accommodates all youth. The suggestions presented in this book will not always be easy to implement. While making adjustments to your religious education program to reach out to youth with special needs, you may encounter a variety of roadblocks and difficulties.

We ask you to continue, like Christ, to say, "Let the children come." We encourage you to remain focused on the important mission of welcoming all, rather than just some, of the youth in your community. In doing so you will change the lives of many who, without your efforts, may never experience the joys and the challenges of being a full participant in a Christian community. Your efforts will also affect the lives of parents and catechists. The three reflections that follow illustrate the difference that making changes to meet the needs of youth with neurological differences can make.

Grateful Youth

The following is the response of one student who, in his religious education experience, benefited from many of the suggestions in this book. You might not get to hear a response like the following firsthand from the youth in your community, but it is important to know that, expressed or not, this will be the experience of many of your young people when they feel welcomed in your community:

> Church was really hard for me at first, because I had a hard time following and understanding what they were talking about. I wanted to be a part of it, but it was frustrating to go and sit for such a long time.
>
> It was hard to deal with all the different people and learn about all the teachings, and when it was time for me to be confirmed, I was very nervous and didn't think I could do it.

When it came time for the first meeting, I didn't want to go, and was very tired and putting my own needs before God. When I got there, I couldn't sit still and wanted to leave. I was in a very grumpy mood and made my mom and dad frustrated. I think I embarrassed them as well. It is hard for me to live my life when my problems and frustrations inflict [sic] other people. I yelled at Mom and Dad that day, and I feel really bad about it.

I just didn't fit in with the other kids. They were regular teenagers talking about teenage things like phones and sports, and I was more quiet and "listeny."

My Confirmation teacher at first didn't really understand how hard it was for me. It was hard to be patient and stay calm when I tried to explain it to him. It took a lot of time till he understood. But then he became more and more understanding about my beliefs and the way I need help for him to teach me. He treated me more and more like an individual, thinking about me, rather than teaching us all like we were one person. He let my dad and my brother come with me sometimes, and he let me stand up and walk around when I got antsy.

It was still hard for me to understand things about God, and it was hard to remember all the answers and stuff I read in the Bible and other books. It was a very difficult experience in my case, and I think I made it frustrating for my dad to come there and stay with me.

I sometimes complained about having to go, but when I look back, I realize it was foolish of me to do that. But I did it, and after I finished, I was very proud of the progress I made and the accomplishments.

On my Confirmation day, I saw my mom smile in the audience, and it made my heart feel very . . . comfortable. It was very warming to know that I had a lot of people supporting me through this tough time.

We still go to church. It's an important part of my life, because it's like I have a whole big family there that understands me. With my whole family there, it's very comfortable.

If things didn't work out for me at church, I think I really wouldn't be interested in God, and wouldn't appreciate him, and blame things on God, for not helping me and stuff. I now feel a part of God, and I feel like I'm beside him instead of behind him.

Grateful Parents

One aspect of making accommodations for youth with special needs that might get overlooked is how the changes can affect entire families. When you make changes to help a young person feel welcomed and valued, you are also telling the entire family it is welcomed and valued. Rebecca, the parent of a student at The Monarch School, expressed this beautifully, as follows:

> It is a mixed blessing to go to church with a teenager who has special needs. As a mother of three teenage sons (the eldest of whom, Tommy, has Asperger's syndrome) and one preteen daughter, I can say that it's a challenge even just to get there at times!
>
> There are often behavioral challenges to navigate with a teen on the autistic spectrum, and that can add a stressful element to the morning. Despite these challenges I know there are many benefits to our regular attendance as a family. And not just entertainment for the other parishioners watching our brood nearly wrestling in the pews!
>
> As often as I am concerned that my kids are a distraction, I am greeted with nothing but support from the community. Many know about our son and his special needs and are interested in how he is doing and how we are managing. There are many times when I want to answer, "Barely!" But that wouldn't be accurate.
>
> Tommy has had a difficult time at church. He finds it hard to connect with the other kids. We were concerned that we might have to pull him out. But the church leaders were open to running experiments, trying to help Tommy find places where he feels at home. After a while we found several programs in which Tommy could shine, along with continuing to practice in more difficult settings with kids his own age. He is routinely commended for his patience with young kids, and it warms my heart when I am told that Tommy is doing great helping out in the pre-K group! Or, so polite when he serves the seniors of the parish (like when he clears the dishes for seniors at a parish supper)! I know this is Tommy at his best, and I am so thankful there are places in our parish where his unique gifts can shine. It is not always a smooth road to church, and there are often angry outbursts en route, but knowing that there is still a place for him makes all the difference.

You too can make a huge difference in the lives of families. Remember that their lives are already challenging. Normal activities like a trip to the grocery store can turn into painful ordeals. You have the power to create an oasis for these youth and their families in your community. With a lot of acceptance and love, and with a little bit of accommodation, you can make it possible for youth to feel a real sense of belonging.

Grateful Catechists

There is an equally great effect on your catechists and volunteers when your religious education program changes to accommodate the special needs youth. It is common for catechists and volunteers to feel frustrated or ill equipped when they have a student with special needs in their classes. They can quickly discover that the traditional ways of teaching do not work, but the catechists do not have the knowledge, resources, or energy to uncover new methods. When you provide catechists the tools to minister to all the youth in the program, you affirm the catechists as volunteers and members of your church. One volunteer catechist expressed it as follows:

When we met with our director for the first time, she told us how excited she was that we were starting a CCE class that included kids with special needs. She had a great reception from the parents about it—she'd been contacted several times in the past few years by parents who wanted to enroll their children in classes but were discouraged by the fact that we didn't offer accommodations for kids with special needs. Some of the kids who are in our class now had tried participating in CCE before, and it hadn't worked well for them: the material wasn't being presented in ways they could follow or identify with, they weren't getting the individual support they needed, or it was just too hard for them to stay focused. Many of them, however, had never been in a CCE class before, because their parents had felt that they couldn't handle it and they didn't even want to try it.

The first few weeks of class were difficult. My co-teacher and I were extremely nervous, although I think some of the parents were more nervous than we were. The director had given them permission to sit in with their kids to see how the class would run and to support them, so for the first few weeks, we had some parents join us. On the fourth week, one of the parents left her son, George, who has autism, alone in the class for the first time. George arrived before I did that day, and I was surprised when I arrived to see that his mom was not there with him. I asked my co-teacher where she was, and she asked George to explain the situation to me. He gave me a big smile and said: "My mom wants me to do good by myself. I have to use my brain to think and slow down." George worked so hard during that class, answering questions, accepting prompts when he got off task, and being very reflective about his own thoughts and behaviors.

At the end of every class, we take time to sit down with each child and reflect on how they did in class that day and what they learned. On this day, George was able to recount to me what we had talked about that day, and he couldn't wait to tell his mom about what we had done. When his mom came to pick George up, she looked very worried as she asked, "How did he do?" We told her how proud we were of George, and we showed her his reflection sheet and the craft he had made. He wasn't disruptive, he stayed on task—and it was like his mother couldn't believe it. She kept asking, "No, *really*, how did he do?" It's amazing how quickly he and all the kids have picked up on the language we use in class and the format we follow, even though many had never been in CCE before. It has also been fun to see George's mom react to his success—she was proud of him that day, and I think it was one of the first times she thought he would really be successful in CCE.

Teaching CCE has become one of the highlights of my week. My students are sweet, bright, and eager to learn. They are always willing to participate and to share their thoughts and feelings. As they get more familiar with one another, we are building our own faith-sharing community, and that is amazing to see. They make sure everyone is included in class activities, and we share a lot of joy and laughter together.

Teaching this class has made me much more aware of the challenges our students face and the difficulty their families have finding adequate services that meet their needs. It seems sad to me that they have encountered these difficulties in a religious setting that is supposed to be very welcoming. I hope the kids in our class will be able to apply the things we learn in class to their lives outside of CCE as well. We use a lot of pacing strategies and guided self-talk that I think could really help them in school.

I hope they will be able to attend Mass and to understand and appreciate what is happening. It's also great to know that we are providing a service to these families that would not otherwise be available. I know the children's families will be excited to see them welcomed into the church community more fully. It is something the whole family can share and an achievement the kids (and we teachers!) can really be proud of. I plan on teaching this class again, and on advocating for it in the parish. I wonder what will happen to our kids after this year though. I hope that in the future, classes like ours will be offered to kids of all ages!

May God Continue to Bless Your Ministry

Congratulations and blessings on your efforts to respond to the Great Commission by reaching out to everyone, regardless of his or her differences. On the journey of ministry to youth with special needs, you will encounter many difficulties. You will, however, also experience amazing moments of witnessing previously excluded young people embracing and living their faith. The gift each child is to your community is immense. By ensuring a place for all, you will bless your community in unforeseeable ways. If on the journey you need assistance, please feel free to contact us at The Monarch School. We would be delighted to support you in this important work. In conclusion consider the following wise words of Charleen Katra, associate director of continuing Christian education in the Archdiocese of Galveston-Houston:

> It's a baptismal right to be included in your faith. It's not based on your abilities; it's your right as a baptized person. I know that the families are extremely grateful for the inclusion of their children in the church, because I know in the past that wasn't always the case. This generation is having a much more positive experience than past generations did in that respect. We can't do enough for these families, but we're going to keep doing all we can.

Acknowledgments

The scriptural quotations contained herein are from the New Revised Standard Version of the Bible, Catholic Edition. Copyright © 1993 and 1989 by the Division of Christian Education of the National Council of the Churches of Christ in the United States of America. All rights reserved.

The quotation on page 14 is from the movie *Star Trek II: The Wrath of Khan*, directed by Nicholas Meyer (Paramount Pictures, (1982).

The story of Moses on page 21 is adapted from the midrash for Exodus and described in "The Making of a Concerned Jewish Leader," by Rabbi Ephraim Buchwald, at *www.njop.org/html/SHEMOT5763-2002.htm*, accessed March 16, 2008.

The symptoms of ADD/ADHD described on page 36 are adapted from the *Diagnostic and Statistical Manual of Mental Disorders: DSM–IV*, fourth edition, text revision by the American Psychiatric Association (Washington, DC: American Psychiatric Association, 2000), page 92. Copyright © 2000 by the American Psychiatric Association. Reprinted with permission.

The quotation by Abraham Lincoln on resource 5–B is from the Abraham Lincoln Research Site, at *home.att.net/~rjnorton/Lincoln84.html*, accessed March 16, 2008.

The information about Dan Aykroyd on resource 5–B is from "Comedian— and Writer—Dan Aykroyd," on the *Fresh Air* radio program, National Public Radio, November 22, 2004.

The quotation by John Nash on resource 5–B is from an interview at *www.schizophrenia.com/sznews/archives/001617.html*, accessed March 16, 2008.

The quotations by Jean-Claude Van Damme on resource 5–B are from *bipolar.about.com/cs/celebs/a/jeanclaude.htm*, accessed March 16, 2008.

The excerpt by Marshall McLuhan on page 72 and the quotation on page 83 are found at *www.brainyquote.com/quotes/quotes/m/marshallmc391513.html*, accessed March 16, 2008.

The nine intelligences listed on page 73 are from *Intelligence Reframed: Multiple Intelligences for the 21st Century*, by Howard Gardner (New York: Basic Books, 1999), pages 41–43 and 47. Copyright © 1999 by Howard Gardner. All rights reserved.

The excerpt on page 82 is from the Autism Society of America Web site, at *www.autism-society.org/site/PageServer?pagename=about_whatis*, accessed March 16, 2008.

The definitions on pages 83 and 106 are from *The American Heritage Dictionary of the English Language*, fourth edition (Boston: Houghton Mifflin, 2000), found at *www.bartleby.com/61*, accessed March 16, 2008.

The information about the saints on resource 8–A is adapted from "Saints Fun Facts," at the Catholic Online Web site, at *www.catholic.org/saints/fun_facts_arch.php,* accessed March 16, 2008. Copyright © by Catholic Online, *www.catholic.org.* Used with permission of Catholic Online.

The information about bunions on handout 8–A is adapted from "Bunions," at the American Academy of Orthopaedic Surgeons Web site, *orthoinfo.aaos.org/topic.cfm?topic=A00155,* accessed March 16, 2008. Reproduced with permission from C.F. Mosely, editor, *Your Orthopaedic Connection* (Rosemount, IL: American Academy of Orthopaedic Surgeons). Available at *orthoinfo.aaos.org.*

The information about hinges on handout 8–A is adapted from *www.technologystudent.com/joints/hinge1.htm* and *www.dulley.com/diy/dw105.htm,* accessed April 16, 2008.

The information about grasses on handout 8–A is adapted from the Web sites *www.american-lawns.com/grasses/grasses.html,* accessed January 17, 2008. *www.allaboutlawns.com/grass-types/cool-season-grasses.php,* and *www.sharpbro.com/clip010.html,* accessed April 16, 2008.

The lyrics on handout 9–A are from the song "Forgiveness," by Jim Witter and Bobby Tomberlin, on the album *Forgiveness* (Curb Records, 2003). Used with permission of Mike Curb Music (BMI)/CurbSongs (ASCAP).

The 1990 and 1993 autism statistics on page 118 are from the Treatment and Education of Autistic and related Communication-handicapped Children (TEACCH) Autism Program, found on the University of North Carolina Department of Psychiatry Web site, *www.teacch.com/info_primer.html,* accessed March 16, 2008.

The 2000 autism statistic on page 118 is from "Prevalence of Autism Spectrum Disorders—Autism and Developmental Disabilities Monitoring Network, Six Sites, United States, 2000," in the Centers for Disease Control and Prevention *MMWR Surveillance Summaries,* February 9, 2007, at *www.cdc.gov/mmwr/preview/mmwrhtml/ss5601a1.htm,* accessed March 16, 2008.

The 2007 statistic for autism on page 118 is adapted from "Prevalence of Autism Spectrum Disorders—Autism and Developmental Disabilities Monitoring Network, 14 Sites, United States, 2002," in the Centers for Disease Control and Prevention *MMWR Surveillance Summaries,* February 9, 2007, at *www.cdc.gov/mmwr/preview/mmwrhtml/ss5601a2.htm,* accessed March 16, 2008.

To view copyright terms and conditions for Internet materials cited here, log on to the home pages for the referenced Web sites.

During this book's preparation, all citations, facts, figures, names, addresses, telephone numbers, Internet URLs, and other pieces of information cited within were verified for accuracy. The authors and Saint Mary's Press staff have made every attempt to reference current and valid sources, but we cannot guarantee the content of any source, and we are not responsible for any changes that may have occurred since our verification. If you find an error in, or have a question or concern about, any of the information or sources listed within, please contact Saint Mary's Press.